# Cooking
# With Fruit

Photography by Ashley Barber

Food presented and prepared by Voula Kyprianou

Published by Bay Books
61–69 Anzac Parade
Kensington NSW 2033
Publisher: George Barber
Copyright © Bay Books, 1985

National Library of Australia
Card number and ISBN 0 85835 822 0

Designed by Jo Sandford

The publisher wishes to thank the following organis-
ations for their assistance during the photographing
of dishes for this book: Hale Imports Pty Ltd for
Pillvuyt porcelain; Kosta Boda for Fitz and Floyd china
and dinnerware; Saywell Imports for Crown
Corningware; Mikasa Tableware; Suomi for Finlandia
glassware; Baytree Kitchen Shop; and Fred Pazotti Pty
Ltd for tiles.

# Cooking With Fruit

Compiled by
Mary-Lou Arnold

Bay Books
Sydney & London

# CONTENTS

*South Pacific Cold Fruit Soup (see recipe page 23)*

# INTRODUCTION

For many fruit eaters, a fruit cookbook may sound like a contradiction in terms. However, there is a lot more to fruit than fruit salad and cream. In fact fruit has been served as an accompaniment to meat in the western world for centuries: roast pork and apple sauce, beef and redcurrant jelly, cold meat and chutney, and so on.

But this cookbook doesn't stop at sauces, desserts and jams. There are fruit soups, dishes cooked with meat or fish and fruit, fruit with vegetables, rice and salads, fruit breads and many other exotic combinations.

In tropical countries fruit such as coconuts and pineapples are used in traditional cooking and many of these recipes are now used in Australia, thanks to the climate and the influx of settlers from all over the world.

Avocados, mangoes, pawpaws, pineapples, kiwifruit and coconuts have been eaten in this country for years. But with a tropical climate such as ours the possibilities for exotic fruit are boundless. Today feijoas, tamarillos, jackfruit, figs, prickly pears, lychees, guavas, quinces, persimmons, pomegranates and fresh dates are readily available and offer a wealth of material for experimentation in the kitchen.

Fruit lends a tang or a sweetness to many different foods. Having tried the recipes in this cookbook, the adventurous cook may feel inspired to invent other combinations and give family and friends the pleasure of eating something deliciously different.

# HINTS FOR PRESENTATION AND PREPARATION

- Fruit skins make attractive serving dishes and can be balanced on a lettuce leaf, or a bed of lettuce or rice.
- For orange, grapefruit or pineapple cases, remove pulp with a grapefruit knife.
- To segment orange or grapefruit, remove all the white pith and membrane between the segments.
- When grating the rind of citrus fruits, grate only the coloured skin or zest as this is where the flavour is. The white pith under the skin may give a bitter flavour.
- To prepare avocado, cut in half lengthwise. Hit the seed with a sharp cook's knife, twist and pull out the seed. Peel skin from narrow end.
- To open a coconut, pierce two of the 'eyes' and pour out the liquid. Hold coconut in one hand and hit all around, between the eyes and base, with a hammer. Prise the meat out with a knife and pull the skin with a vegetable peeler. Grate the meat in the blender or food processor. Grated coconut may be frozen.

- A coconut yields approximately 4 cups grated coconut.
- To make coconut cream or thick milk, add 2 cups water to 1 cup grated coconut and purée in blender or food processor. Strain through a fine sieve.
- To make coconut milk, add 1 cup water to coconut used for coconut cream and repeat process.
- To peel peaches, cover with boiling water for 1 minute.
- To tenderise meat and octopus, wrap in pawpaw leaves and leave overnight, or rub over with green pawpaw juice.

## NOTES ON BOTTLING
- Use clean jars with no cracks or chips.
- Wash and rinse jars. Line a large saucepan with a cloth to prevent jars from breaking. Place jars in saucepan. Cover with water and boil for 20 minutes. Drain and fill while still warm.
- To seal, use tight lids that have been boiled for 5 minutes. Or, tightly tie waxed or greaseproof paper around neck of jar, using rubber bands.

*Kiwifruit and Nut Salad (see recipe page 25)*

# SEASONAL FRUIT GUIDE:
## when each fruit is at its best

**January**
Apricots, plums, peaches, pears, mangoes, watermelon, grapes, strawberries, figs, avocados, cherries, nectarines, quinces, melons, dates, guavas, tomatoes, lychees

**February**
Pears, quinces, plums, peaches, nectarines, rockmelons, grapes, persimmons, figs, watermelon, apricots, mangoes, blackberries, dates, jackfruit, guavas, tomatoes, lychees

**March**
Apples, pears, quinces, plums, peaches, nectarines, rockmelons, honeydew melons, watermelon, grapes, persimmons, figs, apricots, avocados, custard apples, pawpaws, jackfruit

**April**
Apples, pears, quinces, custard apples, grapes, persimmons, avocados, custard apples, mandarins, pawpaws, peaches, pomegranates

**May**
Apples, pears, pawpaws, custard apples, lemons, feijoas, pomegranates, avocados, kiwifruit, mandarins, persimmons, quinces, tamarillos, coconuts

**June**
Navel oranges, mandarins, apples, pears, pawpaws, custard apples, lemons, feijoas, avocados, kiwifruit, persimmons, tamarillos, coconuts

**July**
Oranges, mandarins, grapefruit, apples, pears, pawpaws, custard apples, strawberries, avocados, kiwifruit, tamarillos, coconuts

**August**
Oranges, grapefruit, mandarins, pears, pawpaws, strawberries, lemons, avocados, kiwifruit, tamarillos, coconuts, cumquats

**September**
Oranges (most varieties), mandarins, grapefruit, apples, pears, pawpaws, strawberries, avocados, kiwifruit, tamarillos, coconuts, cumquats

**October**
Oranges (Valencias), mandarins, lemons, grapefruit, apples, pears, pawpaws (very plentiful), strawberries, watermelon, apricots, avocados, cherries, kiwifruit, peaches, tamarillos, mulberries

**November**
Grapefruit, apples, pears, apricots, cherries, pawpaws, gooseberries, watermelon, avocados, kiwifruit, mangoes, peaches, plums, boysenberries, blackcurrants, raspberries, mulberries, guavas

**December**
Apricots, plums, cherries, peaches, pawpaws, mangoes, watermelon, rockmelon, strawberries, gooseberries, cherries, nectarines, blackcurrants, raspberries, mulberries, dates, guavas, tomatoes

**All year round**
Oranges, lemons, pineapples, passionfruit, bananas, apples, limes, tomatoes

*Curried Cheese Dip for Fruit (see recipe page 12)*

# STARTERS AND PARTY FAVOURITES

## AVOCADO DIP

1 avocado
1 tablespoon chopped stuffed olives
1 teaspoon lemon juice
½ teaspoon finely grated lemon rind
1 small onion, grated
1 clove garlic, crushed
½ teaspoon salt
½ teaspoon paprika
shredded red cabbage for garnish

Wash avocado, cut in half and remove seed. Spoon out flesh and mash with remaining ingredients. Spoon back into shells. Garnish with shreds of red cabbage. Serve with grapes and melon balls.

Makes 1 cup

*left: Avocado Dip*

*Fish Dip for Crudités*

## FISH DIP FOR CRUDITÉS

500 g fish fillets, skinned, boned and steamed
2 limes, peeled and quartered
6 shallots, sliced
4 cloves garlic, peeled
1 red chilli, seeded
2 teaspoons grated ginger
1 teaspoon anchovy sauce
1 teaspoon brown sugar
freshly ground black pepper
selection of raw vegetables and fruit

Mash fish. Roughly chop limes, shallots, garlic, chilli and ginger. Add anchovy sauce and brown sugar and mix by hand or in blender or food processor. Season to taste with pepper. Pile into bowl and allow to stand for at least 1 hour. Serve on platter surrounded by raw vegetables and fruit sliced into bite-sized pieces.

Makes 1½ cups

1   Mash fish

2   Mix in garlic, chilli and grated ginger

3   Serve with chopped raw vegetables and fruit

# CURRIED CHEESE DIP FOR FRUIT

250 g cream cheese
½ cup sour cream
1–2 teaspoons curry powder
1 teaspoon garam masala
1 teaspoon lime juice

Mix all ingredients until smooth and serve with a selection of fruit such as: pawpaw, banana or apple slices, rockmelon balls or strawberries.

Makes 1½ cups

*pictured on page 8*

# HONEYDEW MELON WITH CRAB

2 honeydew melons, halved and seeded
250 g crabmeat
½ cup cream
½ cup mayonnaise
½–1 teaspoon curry powder
mint or parsley for garnish

Scoop all flesh from melons with a melon baller. Mix remaining ingredients together and combine with melon balls. Spoon into melon halves, garnish with mint or parsley and chill thoroughly before serving.

Serves 4

# BAKED AVOCADO SEAFOOD

125 g green prawns, peeled
6 scallops
5 tablespoons butter
6 oysters
3 shallots, chopped
2 tablespoons flour
1 cup fish stock
2 tablespoons chopped parsley
1 teaspoon lemon juice
½ teaspoon Worcestershire sauce
salt
freshly ground black pepper
3 tablespoons cream
3 avocados, halved and seeded
fresh dill for garnish

Gently fry prawns and scallops in 3 tablespoons butter until prawns turn pink. Set aside 6 prawns for garnish. Add oysters and shallots to remaining cooked prawns and set aside. Melt remaining 2 tablespoons butter, stir in flour and cook 2 minutes over low heat. Gradually add stock, stirring constantly. Bring slowly to the boil, stirring and cook until sauce thickens. Add parsley, lemon juice and Worcestershire sauce and season to taste with salt and pepper. Combine with seafood mixture, add cream and spoon into avocado halves.

Bake at 180°C (350°F) for 15 minutes. Garnish with fresh dill and cooked prawns.

Serves 6

*Baked Avocado Seafood*

1   Add shallots to prawns, scallops and oysters

2   Gradually add stock to butter and flour, bring to the boil, stirring until thickened.

3   Finally, stir in cream

# CURRIED AVOCADO BAKE

2 cups fresh white breadcrumbs
90 g butter
4 eggs, hard-boiled and chopped
100 g salami, finely chopped
1 teaspoon French mustard
1½ teaspoons curry powder
½ cup milk
salt
freshly ground black pepper
3 avocados
juice ½ lemon

Toast ½ cup breadcrumbs in 140°C (275°F) oven for 10 minutes.
   Melt half the butter and combine with remaining breadcrumbs, eggs, salami, mustard, curry powder, milk, salt and pepper. Halve avocados and remove seeds. Brush cut surfaces with lemon juice to prevent discoloration.
   Stuff avocados, pressing filling down with back of spoon. Arrange in greased baking dish. Sprinkle avocados with toasted breadcrumbs and dot with remaining butter. Bake at 190°C (375°F) for 25 minutes or until browned on top.

Serves 6

# STUFFED GREEN PAWPAW

1 green pawpaw
1 tablespoon oil
2–3 bacon rashers, finely chopped
1 small onion, finely chopped
1 clove garlic, crushed
1 small red capsicum, finely chopped
2 slices fresh bread, crumbed
1 egg
1 tablespoon cream
salt
freshly ground pepper

Cut stem end off pawpaw and scoop out seeds. Sauté bacon, onion and garlic in oil for 3 minutes. Off the heat, stir in capsicum, breadcrumbs, egg and cream. Season to taste. Stuff into pawpaw, replace stem end and wrap in foil. Bake at 150°C (300°F) for 2½–3 hours until fruit is tender. Serve sliced, hot or cold.

Serves 4

# PAWPAW WITH PRAWNS

3 cups diced, cooked prawns
3 cups grated fresh coconut
2 teaspoons grated fresh ginger
4 pawpaws, peeled, halved and seeded
½ cup lime juice
preserved ginger for garnish

Combine prawns, coconut and ginger. Pile into pawpaw halves. Spoon lime juice over prawn mixture. Garnish with thin slices of preserved ginger.

Serves 8

# LYCHEE COCKTAIL

250 g lychees, peeled, halved and seeded
1 cup diced pineapple
1 cup diced orange
1 tablespoon sugar
2 teaspoons lemon juice

Combine fruits and chill for 1 hour. Add sugar and lemon juice. Serve in chilled cocktail glasses.

Serves 4

# ROCKMELON STUFFED WITH CHEESE

250 g blue vein cheese
250 g cream cheese
¼ cup cream
1 rockmelon, halved and seeded

Thoroughly blend cheeses together. Beat in cream until fluffy. Scoop melon balls from rockmelon. Spoon cheese dip into rockmelon shell. Serve with savoury biscuits and melon balls skewered on toothpicks.

Serves 4

*Rockmelon Stuffed with Cheese*

# PIQUANT FRUIT COCKTAIL

1 pawpaw, peeled and diced
1 cucumber, seeded and diced
1 red capsicum, seeded and chopped

## SAUCE:
1 tablespoon soy sauce
1 tablespoon fresh lime juice
½ cup thick coconut cream
1 fresh red chilli, cut in half and seeded

Shake sauce ingredients together in a screwtop jar and leave for 1 hour. Remove chilli. Mix pawpaw, cucumber and capsicum together, pile into 4 individual serving dishes and pour sauce over. Alternatively, arrange fruits separately in individual serving dishes. Serve well chilled. Sauce may be served separately.

Serves 4

*left:* *Piquant Fruit Cocktail*

# GLACÉ GRAPEFRUIT

2 large grapefruit, halved
1 orange
½ cup caster sugar
4 tablespoons medium sherry
4 strawberries for garnish
mint leaves for garnish
extra orange and grapefruit segments and shredded peel for garnish

Finely grate orange rind. Segment grapefruit and orange and dice. Reserve grapefruit halves. Blend flesh with sugar, sherry and rind. Fill grapefruit halves with mixture and freeze until set. Garnish with orange and grapefruit segments, shredded peel, mint leaves and halved strawberries.

Serves 4

*Glacé Grapefruit*
1  *Dice grapefruit and orange segments*
2  *Blend sugar with fruit, sherry and rind*
3  *Spoon mixture into grapefruit halves and freeze*

# SOUPS

## ROCKMELON SOUP

750 g rockmelon, halved and seeded
200 g seedless grapes
200 g apricots, halved and stoned
1 medium apple, peeled, cored and sliced
1–2 tablespoons lemon juice
3 cups dry white wine
1½ teaspoons cornflour
1 tablespoon honey
75 g pinenuts

Remove flesh from half the rockmelon and dice. Using melon baller, scoop flesh from other half. Simmer diced melon, grapes, apricots, apple, lemon juice and wine for 20 minutes. Allow to cool slightly then purée using a sieve, blender or food processor. Return purée to saucepan. Mix cornflour to paste with a little water. Stir cornflour and honey into soup and cook until slightly thickened. Stir in melon balls and chill thoroughly.

Before serving, toast pinenuts by tossing in frying pan until just starting to brown. Cool. Ladle soup into 6 bowls and sprinkle with pinenuts. Alternatively, arrange melon balls and pinenuts in individual bowls of soup just before serving.

Serves 6

## BLACKBERRY SOUP

4 cups blackberries
1 cup water
1 cup dry white wine
¾ cup sugar
3 large strips lemon rind
1 stick cinnamon
3 whole cloves
1 cup sour cream
1 cup plain yoghurt

Set aside ¼ cup blackberries for garnish. Combine remainder with water, wine, sugar, lemon rind, cinnamon and cloves. Simmer, covered, over low heat, stirring occasionally for 10–15 minutes until soft. Remove lid and allow to cool for 10 minutes. Discard lemon rind, cinnamon and cloves.

Purée mixture in blender or food processor. Chill thoroughly. Just before serving, beat in sour cream and yoghurt until smooth. Garnish with reserved blackberries. Like other fruit soups, this is a rich dish. Half a cup each serve.

Serves 8

*Rockmelon Soup*

1 Add wine to fruit mixture and simmer for 20 minutes

2 After cooling, purée mixture through sieve, blender or food processor

3 Pour cornflour paste and honey into purée and cook until slightly thickened

# WATERMELON SOUP

2 kg watermelon flesh, seeded
500 mL sweet white wine
3 tablespoons honey
½ teaspoon garam masala
grated rind 1 lemon
grated rind and juice 1 orange
300 g sour cream
grated nutmeg and dill sprigs for garnish

Bring watermelon, wine, honey, garam masala and lemon rind to the boil, stirring constantly. Reduce heat and simmer for 20 minutes. Allow to cool. Purée in blender or food processor. Stir in sour cream and chill thoroughly before serving. Garnish with dill sprigs and sprinkle lightly with grated nutmeg before serving.

Serves 6

*Watermelon Soup*

# RASPBERRY SOUP

3½ cups raspberries
¾ cup water
2 tablespoons finely chopped orange rind
juice 1 orange
2 tablespoons cornflour
pinch salt
½ cup sugar
2 cups rosé wine
6 tablespoons sour cream

Set half cup of raspberries aside for garnish. Purée remainder in blender or food processor. Place in medium-mesh sieve set over bowl. Press purée through sieve with back of large spoon; reserve in bowl.

Spoon leftover seeds into small saucepan, add water and stir. Add orange rind and juice and simmer, covered, 5 minutes. Strain mixture into small bowl; discard seeds. Return liquid to saucepan.

Blend cornflour with 2 tablespoons water to make smooth paste, stir into liquid in saucepan until well blended. Heat mixture over low heat, stirring constantly until thickened, about 3 minutes. Stir in salt and sugar until dissolved; stir in raspberry purée and wine until well blended. Chill thoroughly. To serve add spoonful sour cream to each bowl and garnish with reserved raspberries.

Serves 6

*Raspberry Soup*

1   *Press purée through medium-mesh sieve into bowl*

2   *Add orange rind to seeds in water and simmer 5 minutes*

3   *Stir purée and wine until blended with mixture in saucepan*

*Avocado Soup*

1 **Stir flour into melted butter and cook**

2 **Add chopped tomatoes**

3 **Stir in stock and seasoning**

# AVOCADO SOUP

1 tablespoon butter
1 tablespoon flour
½ teaspoon onion juice
2 tomatoes, peeled, seeded and chopped
4 cups beef stock
salt
freshly ground black pepper
3 avocados, peeled, halved and seeded
5 tablespoons cream
croutons made from 3 slices of bread diced and fried

Melt butter, stir in flour and cook for 2 minutes. Add onion juice, tomatoes, stock and season to taste. Bring to boil and cook, stirring, for 10-15 minutes until slightly thickened. Mash avocados with cream and place in soup tureen. Pour soup over avocados. Serve with croutons.

**Serves 8**

# SOUTH PACIFIC COLD FRUIT SOUP

500 g black ripe cherries, stoned
2 peaches, peeled, seeded and thinly sliced
1 stick cinnamon
4 whole cloves
juice 1 lime
4 cups water
3 tablespoons honey
2 tablespoons cornflour
3 tablespoons water
½ teaspoon almond extract
1 cup red wine
½ cup sour cream, 1 sliced lime and ¼ cup slivered, browned
   almonds for garnish

Simmer cherries, peaches, cinnamon, cloves, lime juice, water and honey together in covered saucepan for 15 minutes. Discard cinnamon and cloves. Blend cornflour with water and stir into soup, cooking over low heat until slightly thickened. Stir in almond extract and wine and chill thoroughly.

Spoon fruit evenly into serving plates, pour liquid over and garnish with a dollop of sour cream, slices of lime and almonds.

Serves 6

*pictured on page* 4

# CUSTARD APPLE SOUP

2 medium–size, ripe custard apples
2 cups chicken stock
juice 2 limes
1 cup sour cream
salt
freshly ground pepper
lemon slices and dill sprigs for garnish

Scoop out flesh of custard apples; discard seeds. Purée in blender or food processor, gradually adding stock, until smooth. Blend in lime juice.

Transfer mixture to bowl. Stir in sour cream. Season to taste with salt and pepper. Serve in bowls garnished with lemon slices and dill.

Serves 4

# BLUEBERRY SOUP

2 cups blueberries
1½ cups water
¼ cup sugar
8 cm strip lemon peel
1 stick cinnamon
¾ cup sour cream

Simmer blueberries, water, sugar, lemon peel and cinnamon stick for 15 minutes. Allow to stand for 10 minutes, then discard lemon peel and cinnamon stick. Purée in blender or food processor and chill thoroughly. Just before serving, blend in sour cream. This soup is very rich. Half a cup each serve is sufficient.

Serves 6

# CHERRY SOUP

500 g black ripe cherries, stoned
3 cups water
½ cup sugar
⅓ cup lemon juice
fresh mint or parsley for garnish
plain yoghurt (optional)

Bring cherries, water, sugar and lemon juice to boil. Simmer gently for 10 minutes. Allow to cool. Purée in blender or food processor.

Chill thoroughly. Serve garnished with mint or parsley and, if liked, a teaspoon of yoghurt in each bowl.
NOTE: This recipe may also be served over crushed ice.

Serves 6

*Cherry Soup*

# SALADS AND DRESSINGS

## KIWIFRUIT AND NUT SALAD

1 lettuce
4 kiwifruit, peeled and sliced
2 oranges, peeled and segmented
4 radishes, thinly sliced
100 g button mushrooms, thinly sliced
small cucumber, thinly sliced
1 stick celery, thinly sliced
50 g cashew nuts
vinaigrette dressing (*see recipe following*)
shredded orange peel for garnish

Tear lettuce into pieces. Mix all ingredients together. Make dressing in salad bowl, add salad ingredients and toss with dressing. Alternatively, dressing may be served separately. Garnish with fine shreds of orange peel.

Serves 4–6

### VINAIGRETTE DRESSING:
1 tablespoon Dijon mustard
1 teaspoon salt
freshly ground white pepper
2 tablespoons white wine vinegar
2 teaspoons orange juice
2 tablespoons olive oil

Blend mustard, salt, pepper, orange juice and vinegar together in wooden salad bowl. Blend in olive oil gradually until well mixed.

Makes ½ cup

*pictured on page 6*

## CHICKEN-LYCHEE SALAD

4 chicken breasts
juice 2 limes
1 cup chicken stock
1 bay leaf
250 g lychees, peeled and stoned
2 cups rockmelon balls
1 cup chopped celery
1 cup sour cream
¾ cup lime honey dressing (*see recipe following*)
lettuce leaves
½ cup toasted, slivered almonds for garnish

Marinade chicken in lime juice for 2 hours. Put in saucepan, add stock and bay leaf and simmer for 15 minutes until chicken is tender. Drain, cool and then chop chicken for salad. Toss chicken, fruit and celery with sour cream and dressing. Serve on lettuce and sprinkle with almonds.

Serves 8

### LIME HONEY DRESSING:
grated rind 1 lime
½ cup lime juice
1 tablespoon honey
½ teaspoon salt
½ teaspoon paprika
½ teaspoon French mustard
1 cup salad oil

Shake all ingredients together in screwtop jar and refrigerate.

Makes 1½ cups

*Fish and Fruit Salad (see recipe page 28)*

# APPLE AND DATE SALAD

1 cup stoned, chopped fresh dates
3 cups apples, cored and chopped
½ cup slivered almonds
Californian salad dressing (*see recipe following*)
4 firm lettuce leaves

Mix dates, apples and almonds together with dressing. Pile in lettuce leaf cups.

Serves 4

## CALIFORNIAN SALAD DRESSING:
1 tablespoon Worcestershire sauce
1 tablespoon olive oil
1 teaspoon lemon juice
grated rind ½ lemon

Shake all ingredients together in screwtop jar.

Makes ¼ cup

# CUMQUAT AVOCADO SALAD

1 packet lemon flavoured jelly
½ cup boiling water
1 ¼ cups dry ginger ale
¼ teaspoon salt
2 cups thinly sliced cumquats
2 avocados, peeled, seeded and diced

Dissolve jelly in boiling water. Stir in dry ginger ale and salt. Chill until mixture is slightly thicker than consistency of thick unbeaten egg white. Mix in cumquats and avocados, pour into mould and chill in refrigerator until firm.

To serve, dip mould into hot water, cover with serving platter and tip out.

Serves 6

*Apple and Date Salad*

Florida Salad
1   Mix grapefruit with diced apple
2   Add orange and tomato
3   Pour mayonnaise over fruit and walnuts

# FLORIDA SALAD

2 apples, diced
3 tomatoes, diced
1 grapefruit, peeled and segmented
2 oranges, peeled and segmented
2–3 tablespoons mayonnaise
1 tablespoon sugar
1 tablespoon cream cheese
1 tablespoon chopped walnuts
lettuce leaves

Combine apples, tomatoes, grapefruit and oranges. Mix with remaining ingredients and chill thoroughly. Serve on bed of lettuce. Mayonnaise may be served separately.

Serves 4–6

# GREEN PAWPAW SALAD

5 tablespoons dried shrimp
1 unripe pawpaw, peeled and seeded
5 cloves garlic, peeled
1–2 red chillies, seeded
juice 2 limes
4–5 teaspoons anchovy sauce
4 firm lettuce leaves

Bring water to the boil and soak dried shrimp for at least 30 minutes. Purée all ingredients together in blender or food processor, adding more lime juice and/or anchovy sauce to taste if required. Serve in lettuce cups.

Serves 4

*Pear Salad*

1   Mix together grapes, pineapple and nuts

2   Press fruit and nut mixture into pear halves

3   Blend ingredients for sour cream dressing

# PEAR SALAD

4 large pears, peeled, halved lengthwise and cored
1 cup green grapes, halved and seeded
1 cup chopped pineapple
1 cup chopped walnuts
8 firm lettuce leaves
sour cream dressing (*see recipe following*)

Mix grapes, pineapple and walnuts together and press into pears. Serve in lettuce leaf cups with sour cream dressing.

Serves 8

## SOUR CREAM DRESSING:

1 cup sour cream
2 teaspoons sugar
1 tablespoon lemon juice
½ teaspoon dry mustard
¼ teaspoon paprika
pinch salt

Blend all ingredients together until well mixed.

Makes 1 cup

# FISH AND FRUIT SALAD

500 g white fish fillets
¼ cup lemon juice
3 slices fresh pineapple, diced
6 guavas, stoned and diced
3 bananas, sliced
1 large firm ripe mango, peeled, stoned and diced
1 Spanish onion, thinly sliced
1 red chilli, seeded and finely chopped
¾ cup thick coconut milk
salt    freshly ground black pepper
red capsicum or snipped chives for garnish

Cut fish into narrow strips and marinate in the lemon juice for at least 6 hours. Drain and arrange the fish and prepared fruit in a salad bowl. Garnish with the onion and chilli and pour over coconut milk. Add salt and pepper to taste. Chill thoroughly. Garnish with strips of red capsicum or chives. Coconut milk may be served separately if preferred.

Serves 4

*Fish and Fruit Salad*

1   Marinate fish in lemon juice for 6 hours

2   Add onion and chilli to fruit and fish

3   Pour on coconut milk and mix together

# WATERMELON SALAD

½ watermelon
1–2 rockmelons
3 cups cooked rice
1 large can whole corn kernels
500 g black grapes, peeled and seeded
500 g white grapes, peeled and seeded
mint or basil leaves for garnish

Scoop all the flesh out of the melons using a melon baller. Remove watermelon seeds. Combine all ingredients and pile into watermelon shell. Cover with foil or plastic wrap and chill. Serve garnished with mint or basil leaves. Vinaigrette dressing (*see recipe*) can be poured over salad if desired.

Serves 6–8

# AMBROSIA

1 cup diced orange
1 cup grated coconut
1 cup diced pineapple
1 cup sour cream
1 cup chopped white marshmallows
4 firm lettuce leaves

Mix together and chill. Serve in lettuce leaf cups.

Serves 4

# AVOCADO CREAM DRESSING

1 cup cream
¾ cup mashed avocado
1 tablespoon icing sugar
½ teaspoon salt
½ tablespoon honey
grated rind 1 orange

Whip cream until thick then fold in remaining ingredients. Serve over berry fruits.

Makes 2 cups

# MIMOSA DRESSING

A dressing suitable for vegetables such as artichokes or asparagus, or fruits such as figs, grapes, melons, berry fruits or kiwifruits.

1 tablespoon Dijon mustard
2 tablespoons lemon juice
4 tablespoons olive oil
4 tablespoons salad oil
1 hard-boiled egg, finely chopped
2 tablespoons chopped parsley
salt
freshly ground black pepper

Combine mustard, lemon juice and oils in a screwtop jar and shake until well mixed. Add egg and parsley and season to taste.

Makes ¾ cup

# LEMON DRESSING

Try this one on avocado slices.

2 tablespoons lemon juice
finely grated zest 1 lemon
3 tablespoons olive oil
2 teaspoons rum
½ teaspoon brown sugar
salt
freshly cracked black pepper

Measure all ingredients in screwtop jar and shake to mix well.

Makes ½ cup

*left: Lemon Dressing*

# LEMON YOGHURT DRESSING

An oil-free dressing, ideal for pawpaw, grapes, melons and strawberries.

⅔ cup yoghurt
finely grated rind and juice ½ lemon
1 tablespoon finely chopped parsley
1 tablespoon finely chopped chives
1 tablespoon finely chopped thyme or mint
salt
freshly ground black pepper

Combine all ingredients and mix well. Season to taste.

Makes ⅔ cup

*Lemon Yoghurt Dressing*

# MAIN MEALS

## BANANA AND MUSHROOM STEAK

750 g piece topside steak
2 bananas
1 tablespoon brown sugar
1 teaspoon lemon juice
1 packet mushroom soup
1 tablespoon finely chopped parsley for garnish

Cut pocket in steak. Mash bananas with sugar and lemon juice and fill cavity. Secure opening with skewer. Make mushroom soup using ¾ of the amount of water stated on packet. Place meat in deep casserole and pour in soup. Cover and bake at 150°C (300°F) for 1½ hours until meat is tender. Serve sprinkled with parsley.

Serves 4

*Tropical Steak*

## TROPICAL STEAK

1 kg round steak, cut into strips 1 cm thick
1 tablespoon oil
2 onions, thinly sliced
½ cup rum
⅔ cup pineapple juice
½ cup brown sugar
½ teaspoon finely chopped ginger
2 tablespoons arrowroot
⅓ cup teriyaki sauce
2 tablespoons red wine vinegar
2 tomatoes, peeled and quartered
½ cup sliced button mushrooms
1 avocado, peeled, seeded and cut in strips
1 pawpaw, peeled, seeded and cut into wedges

Brown meat quickly in oil. Add onions and fry for a few minutes. Add rum, cover and simmer for 30 minutes. Add pineapple juice. Blend together sugar, ginger, arrowroot, teriyaki sauce and vinegar and cook, stirring constantly, over low heat until thickened. Stir lightly into meat. Arrange tomatoes, mushrooms, avocado and pawpaw over meat, cover and cook for 10 minutes until heated through.

Serves 6

## BEEF CASSEROLE WITH KIWIFRUIT

1 kg round or topside steak
2–3 kiwifruit, peeled and sliced
1 tablespoon oil
1 onion, sliced
1 red capsicum, sliced
1 tablespoon flour
1 cup beef stock
1 tablespoon soy sauce
1 tablespoon French mustard
cracked black pepper

Rub meat all over with a few slices of kiwifruit to tenderise. Cut meat into 6 pieces and let stand for 10–15 minutes. Brown steaks in hot oil. Remove meat and sauté onions and capsicum in the oil until tender. Stir in flour and allow to brown. Stir in stock, soy sauce, mustard and pepper. Return meat to pan with remaining kiwifruit, cover and simmer over low heat for 1 hour until tender. Serve with buttered pasta.

Serves 6

*pictured on page 35*

*Pineapple Meatballs*

1  Fry meatballs slowly in oil

2  Add remaining vegetables and pineapple to the onion mixture

3  Mix vinegar, sherry, sauces, sugar and water and stir into vegetables

# PINEAPPLE MEATBALLS

1.5 kg minced beef
2 teapsoons mixed dried herbs
1 tablespoon oil
1 teaspoon finely chopped ginger
2 cloves garlic, crushed
1 onion, finely chopped
2 sticks celery, sliced
1 carrot, sliced
1 cucumber, peeled and sliced
1 green capsicum, seeded and sliced
1 pineapple, peeled and diced
½ cup white vinegar
1 tablespoon sherry
1 teaspoon soy sauce
1 teaspoon tomato sauce
1 teaspoon Worcestershire sauce
¼ cup brown sugar
¼ cup water
1 tablespoon cornflour

Season minced beef with mixed herbs; roll into small balls and fry gently in oil until cooked. Lift out and keep warm. Add ginger, garlic and onion and cook for a few minutes. Add remaining vegetables and pineapple and cook for 3 minutes. Combine vinegar, sherry, sauces, sugar and water and stir into vegetables. Add meatballs, bring to boil and simmer 5 minutes. Blend cornflour to paste with a little of the liquid, add to vegetables and stir until liquid thickens.

Serves 8

*Beef Casserole with Kiwifruit*

34

1 Coat diced veal with flour and seasoning mixture

2 Brown veal in oil

3 Pour pomegranate sauce over veal

# VEAL WITH POMEGRANATES

1 teaspoon salt
freshly ground black pepper
1 teaspoon paprika
¼ teaspoon allspice
4 tablespoons flour
1 kg stewing veal, cut in 2.5 cm dice
¼ cup oil
1 large onion, chopped
1 tablespoon tomato paste
juice 3 large pomegranates
1 tablespoon honey
1 cup veal or chicken stock
½ cup chopped celery
½ red capsicum, seeded and thinly sliced
pomegranate seeds and parsley or chives for garnish

Mix salt, pepper, paprika and allspice with flour and use to coat diced veal. Brown veal in oil and transfer to casserole. Sauté onion, add tomato paste, pomegranate juice, honey and stock and mix well. Pour sauce over veal, cover and cook at 150°C (300°F) for 1 hour 45 minutes. Add celery and capsicum and cook further 15 minutes until meat is tender. Garnish with pomegranate seeds and parsley or chopped chives.
**NOTE:** To make pomegranate juice, cut ripe pomegranates in half and squeeze on lemon juicer to crush seeds.

Serves 6

# VEAL IN PAWPAW

2 tablespoons butter
1 onion, finely chopped
1 kg stewing veal, cut in 2 cm dice
1 clove garlic, finely chopped
½ teaspoon finely chopped ginger
2 bay leaves
2 teaspoons curry powder
¼ teaspoon dried thyme
¼ teaspoon dried coriander
4 cups hot veal or chicken stock
¼ cup tomato sauce
2 tablespoons arrowroot
¾ cup cream
1 Granny Smith apple, peeled, cored and finely chopped
¼ cup mango chutney
3 tablespoons grated fresh coconut
4 small pawpaws
extra grated coconut for garnish

Sauté onion in butter. Add veal and sauté until browned. Add garlic, ginger, bay leaves, curry powder, thyme and coriander. Blend well and pour in stock and tomato sauce. Cover and simmer 1½ hours until veal is tender. Lift out meat with slotted spoon. Blend arrowroot and cream with a little sauce. Stir into sauce with apple, chutney and coconut. Bring slowly to the boil and cook, stirring constantly, for 15 minutes. Season to taste and strain over veal.

Cut tops off pawpaws, remove seeds and stuff with veal and sauce mixture. Spoon excess sauce around pawpaws. Place in shallow baking dish, sprinkle with extra coconut and bake at 180°C (350°F) for 10 minutes until pawpaws are tender.

Serves 4

# VEAL WITH LYCHEES

500 g veal fillet, thinly sliced
seasoned flour
1 tablespoon oil
1 tablespoon butter
1 cup dry white wine
1 teaspoon lemon juice
250 g lychees, peeled and stoned
1–2 teaspoons Pernod

Lightly coat veal in seasoned flour and sauté in oil and butter until browned. Pour in white wine and lemon juice, cover and simmer for 10 minutes until tender. Remove meat and keep warm.

Add lychees to sauce and boil until liquid is reduced to 1 cup. Stir in Pernod. Spoon sauce and lychees over meat.

Serves 4

# LAMB KEBABS WITH PAWPAW

½ cup oil
¼ cup lime juice
1 teaspoon ground cummin
½ teaspoon ground coriander
½ teaspoon salt
½ teaspoon cracked black pepper
3 shallots, chopped
3 cloves garlic, crushed
2 zucchini, sliced
750 g lamb, cut in 3.5 cm cubes
½ pawpaw, cubed
1 punnet cherry tomatoes
1 lime, thinly sliced

Shake oil, lime juice, cummin, coriander, salt, pepper, shallots and garlic together in screwtop jar. Pour over zucchini, lamb and pawpaw and let stand 30 minutes, turning occasionally. Remove zucchini and lamb from marinade and arrange alternately on skewers. Grill or barbecue zucchini and lamb for 12–15 minutes, turning and basting once with marinade. Put pawpaw and tomatoes on skewers and add 4 minutes before lamb is done. Brush with marinade and turn once or twice.

Serves 4

# BRAISED VEAL WITH PLUMS

3 teaspoons butter
2 onions, finely chopped
1 tablespoon finely chopped parsley
½ teaspoon dried thyme
½ teaspoon dried sage
salt
freshly ground black pepper
1 kg red plums, halved and stoned
1 kg boned shoulder of veal
seasoned flour
250 mL veal or chicken stock
250 mL dry white wine
¼ cup port

Grease deep casserole with butter and sprinkle over half the onions. Cover with half the herbs. Mix remaining onion, herbs and salt and pepper to taste with half the plums and stuff cavity of veal. Coat veal in seasoned flour and place in casserole. Mix stock with wine, pour over veal, cover with foil and lid. Bake at 180°C (350°F) for 1 hour. Add remaining plums and cook, covered, for further 15 minutes until meat is tender.

Remove meat and keep warm. Strain sauce and boil liquid until reduced to 1 cup. Mix strained plums with sauce and port and heat through. Serve with sliced meat.

Serves 4

# BAKED QUINCES STUFFED WITH LAMB

6 large quinces
60 g butter
1 onion, finely chopped
500 g lean minced lamb
salt
freshly ground black pepper
½ teaspoon cinnamon
2 tablespoons split peas, cooked
½ cup sugar
½ cup white vinegar

Thinly slice top from each quince and set aside. Scoop out pulp to make cavity. Fry onion until soft in butter. Remove onion and set aside. Fry meat until browned. Season with salt, pepper and cinnamon. Add split peas to meat with onion and mix well. Stuff quinces with this mixture and arrange in shallow pan. Replace quince tops and add enough water to come 3 cm up quinces. Cover, slowly bring water to the boil, reduce heat and simmer gently for 30 minutes until quinces are nearly tender.

Combine sugar and vinegar and baste quinces. Continue simmering for further 15 minutes.

Serves 6

# HAWAIIAN HOTPOT

1 kg mutton chops
1 pineapple, peeled, cored and sliced
225 g tomato purée
425 g can mushrooms in butter sauce
6 shallots, chopped
1 teaspoon dried basil
salt
freshly ground black pepper
1–1½ cups red wine

Trim fat from chops and place in a layer in ovenproof dish. Cover with pineapple slices. Cover with more chops then another layer of pineapple. Mix tomato purée with mushrooms, shallots and basil and season with salt and pepper and spread evenly over pineapple. Add enough wine to barely cover. Bake at 150°C (300°F) for 1½–2 hours until meat is tender.

Serves 6

*Lamb Kebabs with Pawpaw*

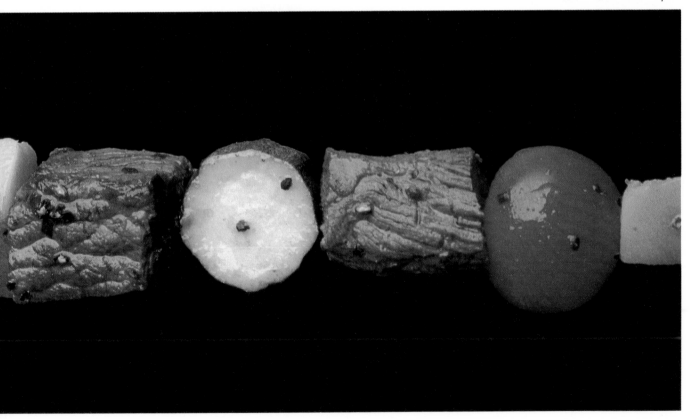

# ORANGES STUFFED WITH MINCED PORK

4 oranges, halved
1 small onion, grated
2 cloves garlic, crushed
2 tablespoons oil
1.25 cm piece ginger, grated
2.5 cm piece lemon grass, finely chopped
500 g lean pork, finely minced
1 tablespoon fish sauce
¼ teaspoon freshly ground black pepper
1 teaspoon sugar
4 tablespoons crushed roasted peanuts
2 tablespoons butter

Use a grapefruit knife to remove all but a thin layer of the flesh from halved oranges to make shells. Discard flesh.

Fry onion and garlic in oil until soft. Grind ginger and lemon grass to a paste with a pestle and mortar. Add to onions and fry for 1 minute. Stir in pork and fry, stirring, until meat is browned. Season with fish sauce, pepper and sugar and cook for 1½–2 minutes.

Spoon into prepared orange shells and smooth over tops. Cover with crushed peanuts, dot with butter and bake at 180°C (350°F) for 30 minutes.

Serves 4

# BRAISED PORK CHOPS WITH PERSIMMON

4 pork chops
2 tablespoons oil
4 spring onions, sliced
1 teaspoon grated ginger
¼ cup white vinegar
½ cup chicken stock
⅓ cup persimmon jam (*see recipe Jams and Chutneys section*)
2 tablespoons soy sauce
1 teaspoon finely sliced ginger and 1 teaspoon finely sliced shallots for garnish

Sauté pork chops in oil for 12 minutes until well browned. Set aside. Pour off excess fat and fry spring onions and ginger for 1 minute. Pour in vinegar, stirring, and boil until liquid reduces to 1 tablespoon. Add stock, persimmon jam and soy sauce and cook, stirring constantly for 7 minutes. Return chops to pan, cover and simmer over low heat for 20 minutes until chops are cooked. Serve garnished with ginger and shallots.

Serves 4

*Braised Pork Chops with Persimmon*
1   *Sauté pork chops in oil until browned*

2   *Add white vinegar to spring onions and ginger, boiling until reduced*

3   *Combine stock, persimmon jam and soy sauce and cook, stirring continuously*

*Braised Pork Chops with Persimmon*

## Mexican Pork and Chicken Casserole

1  Brown the cubed pork in oil and butter

2  Add onions and capsicums to almonds and sesame seeds

3  Combine purée with stock, honey, wine and seasoning

# MEXICAN PORK AND CHICKEN CASSEROLE

500 g lean pork loin, cut in cubes
1 tablespoon oil
1 tablespoon butter
2.5 kg chicken, jointed
1 tablespoon blanched almonds
3 teaspoons sesame seeds
1 onion, finely chopped
1 green capsicum, seeded and finely chopped
1 cup tomato sauce
4 cups chicken stock
1 tablespoon chilli powder
2 tablespoons honey
3 tablespoons dry white wine
¼ teaspoon cinnamon
3 whole cloves
1 bay leaf
1 teaspoon salt
1 sweet potato, peeled and diced
1 apple, peeled, cored and diced
1 cup diced pineapple
2 bananas
parsley to garnish

Brown pork in hot oil and butter. Remove with slotted spoon. Brown chicken in same pan. Remove. Lightly fry almonds and 1 teaspoon sesame seeds in same pan. Stir in onion and capsicum. Sauté a few minutes more. Add tomato sauce and purée in blender or food processor. Combine puréed mixture with stock, chilli, honey, wine, cinnamon, cloves, bay leaf and salt. Cook for 15 minutes. Strain. Return meat to pan, pour over sauce and simmer for 45 minutes. Add sweet potato and simmer for 15 minutes. Add apple and pineapple and simmer for further 10–15 minutes. Just before serving, slice bananas into stew and sprinkle with remaining sesame seeds and finely chopped parsley.

Serves 8

# GRILLED PORK CHOPS WITH PINEAPPLE SAUCE

4 pork chops
1 cup crushed pineapple
½ cup sugar
½ cup white vinegar
½ teaspoon cinnamon
6–8 whole cloves

Grill chops until cooked and keep warm. Simmer pineapple and sugar together for 15 minutes until tender. In separate saucepan, simmer vinegar, cinnamon and cloves for 10 minutes. Strain sauce, mix with pineapple and serve with chops.

Serves 4

# CHICKEN WITH GREEN MANGO CURRY

1 x 1.5 kg chicken, jointed
1 green mango, peeled, seeded and diced
1 cup chicken stock
½ teaspoon salt
¾ teaspoon turmeric
½ coconut
3 green chillies, seeded
6 cloves garlic, peeled
¼ teaspoon cummin seeds
1 tablespoon ghee
½ teaspoon mustard seeds
3 curry leaves

Cook chicken and mango in stock seasoned with salt and ¼ teaspoon turmeric 45 minutes until tender. Grind coconut, chillies, garlic, ½ teaspoon turmeric and cummin seeds in blender or food processor. Add to chicken and cook 5 minutes. Fry mustard seeds and curry leaves in ghee until mustard seeds begin to splutter. Add to curry. Serve with boiled rice.

Serves 4

# AVOCADO CHICKEN CASSEROLE

2 chicken breasts, halved
¼ cup seasoned flour
2 tablespoons butter
½ cup dry white wine
1 cup ribbon noodles
1 small avocado, peeled, stoned and sliced
1 tablespoon lemon juice

## CHEESE SAUCE:

2 tablespoons butter
5 tablespoons flour
½ teaspoon salt
pinch pepper
1½ cups cream
¾ cup milk
1 cup grated tasty cheese
paprika

Lightly coat chicken with seasoned flour and brown in butter. Pour over wine, cover and simmer for 30–40 minutes until tender. If necessary add stock or more wine during cooking. Cool slightly, remove skin and bones and slice chicken. Cook noodles. Prepare avocado and paint with lemon juice.

To make cheese sauce, melt butter, stir in flour, salt and pepper and cook 2 minutes. Off the heat, gradually stir in cream and milk. Heat till boiling, stirring constantly. Remove from heat. Add cheese and stir until melted. Set aside 1 cup sauce and mix remainder with noodles.

Arrange chicken pieces over bottom of lightly greased ovenproof dish. Spoon noodle mixture over chicken. Arrange avocado over noodles and spoon over reserved sauce. Sprinkle lightly with paprika and bake at 180°C (350°F) 25 minutes.

Serves 4

# CHICKEN IN PAWPAW SAUCE

4 chicken breasts, halved and boned
3 tablespoons seasoned flour
1 tablespoon oil
2 tablespoons butter
500 g pawpaw, peeled, seeded and sliced
1 tablespoon honey
1 tablespoon French mustard
1 teaspoon finely chopped preserved ginger
¼ teaspoon dried tarragon
1 cup dry white wine
½ cup cream
salt
freshly ground black pepper
pawpaw slices, olives and finely sliced green capsicum for garnish

Roll chicken fillets in flour and fry in hot oil and butter until brown both sides. Add pawpaw, cover and simmer for 10 minutes; stir in honey, mustard, ginger, tarragon and wine. Bring back to boil, cover and simmer for a few minutes. Lift out chicken and keep warm. Purée pawpaw sauce in blender or food processor. Return to pan, stir in cream, season to taste and serve over chicken garnished with pawpaw slices, olives and sliced capsicum. Serve with fresh green salad.

NOTE: For extra zing, marinate the pawpaw slices for garnish in lemon juice.

Serves 6–8

*Chicken in Pawpaw Sauce*

1   *Fry floured chicken fillets in oil and butter until browned*

2   *Add pawpaw, cover and cook gently for 10 minutes*

3   *Stir honey, mustard, ginger, tarragon and wine into chicken and pawpaw*

1  Brush butter over chicken pieces and place in oven for 35–40 minutes

2  Add sugar to orange and lemon juices and soy sauce

3  Combine cornflour paste with juice and soy sauce mixture

# POLYNESIAN BAKED CHICKEN

1 x 1.5 kg chicken, jointed
½ cup seasoned flour
125 g butter
½ cup orange juice
1 tablespoon lemon juice
2 teaspoons soy sauce
¼ cup brown sugar
2 teaspoons cornflour
½ pineapple, cubed
½ pawpaw, cubed
2 tablespoons finely chopped parsley and 2 tablespoons sesame seeds for garnish

Coat chicken with flour. Grease ovenproof dish with butter and melt remaining butter. Brush over chicken. Bake at 180°C (350°F) for 35–40 minutes until just tender.

Combine orange and lemon juices, soy sauce and sugar and bring to boil, stirring constantly. Make a paste with cornflour and water, add, stirring, and cook until thickened. Add fruit, spoon over chicken and bake further 10 minutes. Garnish with parsley and sesame seeds.

Serves 4

# CHICKEN WITH PEACHES

4 peaches, halved and stoned
2 teaspoons caster sugar
¼ teaspoon grated nutmeg
150 mL white wine
2 X 1 kg chickens
2-3 tablespoons seasoned flour
4 thin slices lemon
4 bacon rashers
125 g butter
8 small mushrooms
150 mL chicken stock
4 tablespoons cream
salt
freshly ground black pepper

Arrange peaches in shallow ovenproof dish, cut side up. Sprinkle with sugar and nutmeg and pour over the wine. Leave standing while chicken is prepared.

Rub chicken all over with seasoned flour. Put a slice of lemon on each side of breast and cover each chicken with 2 rashers of bacon. Dot all over with half the butter. Bake both chicken and peaches at 190°C (375°F) for 35–45 minutes until tender.

Meanwhile prepare the mushrooms. Remove stalks and wipe over caps. Sauté in remaining butter. Heat stock.

Halve chickens and arrange on serving platter surrounded by peach halves. Place mushroom in each peach half and keep hot. Stir cream into pan in which chickens were cooked, add stock and wine from peaches. Stir, season to taste, spoon over chicken and serve immediately.

Serves 6

*Polynesian Baked Chicken*

# CHICKEN BREAST WITH PEARS

2 chicken breasts, halved
4 tablespoons butter
3 spring onions, very finely chopped
1 large pear, peeled, cored and sliced
¾ cup cider
¼ cup calvados
salt
freshly ground black pepper
1 cup cream
fresh herbs, for garnish

Sauté chicken and spring onions in butter over a low heat for 10 minutes. Gently poach pear slices in cider for about 15 minutes until soft but not mushy. Drain pears and set aside. Pour calvados over chicken and ignite. When flame burns out season with salt and pepper then add cream and poaching liquid. Bring to boil and allow to continue just on the boil until liquid is reduced by nearly half. Lift out chicken, arrange on platter, top with pear slices, spoon sauce over and lightly brown under hot grill. Serve with boiled pasta.

Serves 4

*Chicken Breast with Pears*

# FRIED CHICKEN WITH RUM AND LIME

1 x 2 kg chicken, jointed
¼ cup rum
¼ cup freshly squeezed lime juice
¼ cup soy sauce
½ cup flour
½ teaspoon salt
¼ teaspoon freshly ground black pepper
pinch cayenne pepper
pinch paprika
oil for deep frying
juice 2 limes

Place chicken pieces in large bowl. Heat rum in small saucepan to warm then set alight. Shake pan until flames finish. Add ¼ cup lime juice and soy sauce then pour over chicken. Allow to marinate 4–6 hours, turning chicken occasionally. Drain and pat dry.

Combine flour, salt, pepper, cayenne pepper and paprika in large bag, add chicken pieces and shake to coat.

Deep fry chicken in hot oil for about 25 minutes until cooked, turning occasionally. Drain, sprinkle with juice of 2 limes and serve immediately.

Serves 4

# DUCK WITH GRAPE SAUCE

1 x 2 kg duckling
2 tablespoons butter

## GRAPE SAUCE:
¼ cup juice from roasting pan
500 g white grapes
1 tablespoon port
1 teaspoon dried rosemary or sprig fresh rosemary
1 clove garlic, crushed
2 tablespoons juice from jar of maraschino cherries
½ teaspoon salt
freshly ground black pepper
1 tablespoon cream

Rub butter over duck and bake at 180°C (350°F) for 1 hour until tender, basting and turning every 15 minutes.

To make grape sauce, peel grapes and reserve 24 for garnish. Crush remainder and place in saucepan with all other ingredients except cream. Bring to boil and continue boiling for approximately 10 minutes to reduce sauce. Remove from heat, cover and leave standing until duck is ready to serve. Carve bird and arrange on serving platter. Add whole grapes to sauce, heat through. Stir in cream and spoon over duck.

Serves 4

*Coral Island Fish*

1   *Poach fish fillets in wine and cream until tender*

2   *Combine coconut and oysters with banana and tomatoes*

3   *Add egg yolks off heat then return to low heat and stir until thickened*

# CORAL ISLAND FISH

1 kg lean white fish fillets
150 mL Sauterne wine
600 mL cream
2 bananas, sliced
2 tomatoes, peeled and chopped
12 oysters
⅓ cup grated fresh coconut
4 egg yolks
juice ½ lemon
salt
freshly ground black pepper

Poach fish in wine and cream until tender. When cooked, remove from sauce and keep hot. Add bananas, tomatoes, oysters and coconut to liquid and boil for 1 minute. Remove from heat, add egg yolks and stir over low heat until sauce is thickened. Season with lemon juice, salt and pepper, spoon over fish.

Serves 6

*Trout with Apples*

# TROUT WITH APPLES

2 trout
2–3 tablespoons flour
½ cup butter

## SAUCE:
¼ cup slivered almonds
1 large Granny Smith apple, peeled, cored, thinly sliced
2 tablespoons brown sugar
2 tablespoons cream
2–3 sprigs dill for garnish

Lightly coat trout with flour. Heat butter in large frying pan and when sizzling cook trout for 4–5 minutes each side until flesh is white. Drain, reserving butter, and keep warm.

Sauté almonds in reserved butter for 2–3 minutes until golden. Drain. Add apples and cook for 2 minutes; drain. Pour off all but 2 tablespoons butter. Stir brown sugar into pan until dissolved. Stir in cream and heat through.

Arrange almonds and apples over fish then spoon over the sauce. Garnish with dill sprigs.

Serves 2

49

# FRIED WHOLE SNAPPER WITH PINEAPPLE SAUCE

1 x 1.5 kg whole snapper
½ teaspoon salt
1 tablespoon soy sauce
3 tablespoons cornflour
1 egg, beaten
¼–½ cup dried breadcrumbs
oil for deep frying

## SAUCE:

1 pineapple, peeled, sliced then cut into small triangles
2 tablespoons sugar
1 tablespoon white vinegar
½ teaspoon salt
1 tablespoon cornflour

## GARNISH:

Remaining pineapple pieces
1 egg, beaten
¼ cup dried breadcrumbs
1–2 tablespoons oil
½ green capsicum, thinly shredded
½ red capsicum, thinly shredded
2 shallots formed into flowers and soaked in iced water

Score skin of snapper in large diamond shapes. Sprinkle with salt and brush over with soy sauce. Lightly coat with cornflour, brush with egg and coat with breadcrumbs.

Fill ⅓ of a large wok with oil and heat until hot enough to sizzle a piece of bread. Slide fish in head first, allow the thick part of fish to cook for 5–7 minutes then push in tail end to cook for a few minutes. Lift out using two Chinese strainers and allow to drain in kitchen paper. Keep warm.

Put sugar and half the pineapple in a saucepan and barely cover with boiling water. Simmer for 3–5 minutes until pineapple is softened. Add vinegar and salt. Bring to the boil and thicken with cornflour blended to a paste with water. Cook for 2 minutes.

Coat remaining half of pineapple pieces in cornflour, egg, then breadcrumbs. Deep fry in hot oil.

Blanch capsicum strips in boiling water for 1 minute then drain.

Spoon sauce over fish and garnish with fried pineapple, capsicum shreds and shallot flowers.

**Serves 4**

# FILLETS OF SOLE WITH CRANBERRIES

1 cup cranberries
½ cup water
1 tablespoon sugar
5 tablespoons butter
250 g mushrooms, finely chopped
3 tablespoons finely chopped shallots
2 tablespoons finely chopped parsley
6 fillets of sole, skinned
salt
freshly ground black pepper
½ cup port
1 cup fish stock
¼ teaspoon dried tarragon
1 cup cream
2 tablespoons chopped pistachios for garnish

Simmer cranberries, water and sugar for 10 minutes. Allow to cool slightly then purée in food processor or blender. Melt 2 tablespoons butter in frying pan. Sauté mushrooms and shallots, stirring, for 3 minutes. Add parsley and cook, stirring, for further 2 minutes.

Sprinkle skinned side of fish fillets lightly with salt and pepper. Combine cranberry purée and mushroom mixture and spread evenly over fillets. Loosely roll up fillets and secure with toothpicks.

Melt remaining 3 tablespoons butter in large frying pan. Add fish rolls, leaving space between them. Add port and stock, cover and simmer gently for 10 minutes until tender. Remove fish rolls with slotted spoon to warm serving plate and keep warm.

Bring poaching liquid to boil, add tarragon and boil for 5 minutes or until liquid is reduced by half. Add cream and boil for further 5 minutes until liquid is reduced to quarter original amount and sauce lightly coats back of spoon. Spoon sauce over fish rolls, sprinkle with pistachios. Serve immediately.

**Serves 6**

# FISH IN MANGO SAUCE

1½ teaspoons ghee
1 large onion, finely sliced
1 tablespoon cornflour
1 cup water
150 mL mango pulp (1–2 mangoes puréed)
1 kg jewfish, cut in 2.5 cm slices
salt
1–2 tablespoons chopped coriander leaves for garnish

## MASALA PASTE:

1 tablespoon coriander seeds
6 cloves garlic
2 red chillies, seeded
2.5 cm piece ginger
2.5 cm piece coconut

Grind all masala paste ingredients together in blender or food processor.

Heat ghee and fry masala paste for a few minutes. Add onion and fry, stirring for 3–4 minutes. Blend cornflour to a paste with a little water then stir in remaining water. Add to onion and stir well. Add mango pulp and bring to boil, stirring frequently. Add fish and salt to taste. Simmer over low heat for 15–20 minutes until fish is tender. Garnish with coriander.

Serves 4

# SCALLOPS WITH GRAPES

750 g scallops
2 cups seedless green grapes, peeled
1 cup reserved prawn stock (*see recipe* Prawn Cutlets with Plum Sauce) or fish stock
½ cup cream
salt and pepper to taste
parsley sprigs for garnish

Poach scallops and grapes in stock for 8–10 minutes until scallops are just tender. Drain, reserving liquid, and keep warm. Reduce liquid to ¾ cup. Add cream and pour over scallops and grapes. Garnish with parsley sprigs and serve with chunks of bread to soak up the juices.

Serves 4

# PRAWN CUTLETS WITH PLUM SAUCE

1 kg green king prawns
2 egg whites, lightly beaten
¼–½ cup cornflour
oil for deep frying

## SAUCE:
500 g ripe red plums, stoned
100 mL water
⅓–½ cup brown sugar, tightly packed
2 tablespoons tomato sauce
2 teaspoons soy sauce
1–2 teaspoons arrowroot or cornflour
coriander or parsley for garnish

Remove head and shells from prawns leaving tails intact. Reserve heads and shells to make stock. Slit prawns down the back and remove black veins. Continue the split without cutting right through. Open prawns out and flatten lightly with knife to make cutlets. Dip in egg white then coat with cornflour. Deep fry in hot oil for a few minutes until lightly coloured.

To make plum sauce, bring plums and water to the boil and simmer for 5–8 minutes over low heat until just tender. Purée fruit in food processor or push through a fine sieve. Return to pan with brown sugar, tomato sauce and soy sauce. Boil until liquid is reduced to 1½ cups, stirring occasionally.

Stir arrowroot to a paste with a little water then add to sauce. Cook, stirring until thickened.

Serve sauce in a bowl on a platter surrounded by prawn cutlets. Garnish with coriander.
**NOTE:** To make stock from the prawn heads and shells, wash, cover with water and cook for 20 minutes. Drain and reserve (or freeze) for Scallops with Grapes.

Serves 4

# MAIN MEAL ACCOMPANIMENTS AND STUFFINGS

## HONEY GLAZED BANANAS

6 bananas, peeled
⅓ cup lemon juice
2 tablespoons butter
¼ cup honey

Paint bananas with lemon juice. Melt butter, stir in honey and cook bananas over low heat, turning gently, until hot and glazed.
**NOTE:** Serve at a barbecue or with pork or ham.

Serves 6

*Honey Glazed Bananas
and Pineapple and Potato Fry*

## PINEAPPLE AND POTATO FRY

1 pineapple
4 large potatoes
salt
freshly ground black pepper
125 g butter
4–6 teaspoons fruit chutney

Peel and core pineapple, cut into rounds. Peel potatoes and cut into 1 cm slices the same size as the pineapple.

Gently steam potatoes until just tender. Season with salt and pepper. Fry potatoes until golden. Keep warm. Fry pineapple until browned. Serve one slice of potato on each pineapple slice and top with dab of of fruit chutney.
**NOTE:** Serve with fried ham slices.

Serves 4–6

*Honey Glazed Bananas*
1   *Paint bananas with lemon juice*

2   *Melt butter and stir in honey*

3   *Cook bananas over a low heat until
    evenly glazed*

# MIXED FRUIT RAITA

2 cups yoghurt
2 tablespoons cream
½ mango, diced
½ banana, diced
1 slice pineapple, diced
1 tablespoon finely chopped mint
salt

Whip yoghurt and cream together until smooth. Mix in remaining ingredients. Chill thoroughly.

Serves 6

# MANGO RAITA

½ litre creamy yoghurt
salt
2 mangoes, peeled and diced
1 tablespoon ghee
1 tablespoon mustard seeds
2 red chillies, seeded and finely chopped
½ teaspoon fenugreek seeds
chopped coriander for garnish

Whip yoghurt and season with salt. Add mangoes. Heat ghee and fry mustard seeds, chillies and fenugreek until they start to crackle. Strain over yoghurt mixture. Mix together gently with a fork and garnish with chopped coriander.

Serves 6

# BANANA RAITA

2 cups creamy yoghurt
1 teaspoon garam masala
½ teaspoon salt
2 green chillies, seeded and finely chopped
3 bananas, chopped
2 teaspoons ghee
1 teaspoon mustard seeds
chopped coriander for garnish

Flavour yoghurt with garam masala and salt. Mix in green chillies and bananas. Heat ghee in small saucepan and fry mustard seeds until they begin to crackle. Pour over raita and garnish with coriander.

Serves 6

# FRIED JACKFRUIT

500 g jackfruit, peeled and chopped
½ cup water
6 cloves garlic, chopped
½ onion, chopped
2 green chillies, seeded and chopped
2 red chillies, seeded and chopped
1 stick cinnamon
2.5 cm piece ginger, grated
½ cup lentils
1 teaspoon salt
1 teaspoon black peppercorns
½ teaspoon cummin seeds
1 tablespoon chopped coriander leaves
oil for deep frying

Combine all ingredients except coriander and oil and cook until tender and almost dry. Grind to paste in food processor or blender. Mix in coriander. Form into small balls and deep fry.

Serves 4

# JACKFRUIT BHARTHA

1 tender jackfruit, peeled and diced
1 teaspoon turmeric
1 teaspoon salt
½ coconut, grated
1 teaspoon chilli powder
2 tablespoons ghee
1 teaspoon mustard seeds
6 green chillies, seeded and chopped
3 curry leaves
2 tablespoons chopped coriander leaves for garnish

Cook jackfruit, including seeds, in enough water to barely cover it, with turmeric and salt until tender. Mash with fork (including seeds as these have special flavour). Mix in coconut and chilli powder.

Heat ghee and fry mustard seeds, chillies and curry leaves until mustard seeds start to splutter. Add jackfruit mixture and cook 10–15 minutes longer. Garnish with coriander leaves.

Serves 4

*Mango Raita, Banana Raita* and *Mixed Fruit Raita*

Lime Rice

1 Mix lime juice, coconut, turmeric and salt with cooked rice

2 Combine cashew nuts with curry leaves and green chillies

3 Mix chopped coriander leaves with rice and cook slowly for 15 minutes

# PAWPAW VERSATILITY

**Boiled:** Select firm pawpaw and cook, without peeling, in boiling salted water for about ½ hour until tender. Halve, remove seeds, cut into serving-size pieces and dot with butter. Serve with a white sauce.

**Baked:** Select unripe pawpaw, leave skin on, halve, remove seeds and bake with other vegetables for about ½ hour until tender.

# PINEAPPLE PILAU

½ teaspoon saffron
½ cup warm milk
2 pineapples, peeled, cored and diced
1 cup sugar
½ cup water
½ cup ghee
1 tablespoon garam masala
2 cups long grain rice
boiling water
¼ teaspoon salt
1 tablespoon ground almonds

Soak saffron in milk and set aside. Simmer pineapple with sugar in water until thick syrup is formed.

Melt ghee, stir in garam masala and fry for a few minutes. Stir in rice until coated with ghee, add sufficient boiling water so it comes 2.5 cm above rice, season with salt, cover and simmer for 15–20 minutes until all liquid is absorbed. Stir in pineapple and syrup. Add almonds to saffron and milk and pour over rice.

Serves 4

# LIME RICE

2 cups rice, cooked
juice 4–5 limes
½ coconut, grated
1 teaspoon turmeric
½ teaspoon salt
¾ cup ghee
½ cup mustard seeds
1 cup cashews, chopped
2 curry leaves, chopped
6 green chillies, seeded and chopped
1 tablespoon finely chopped coriander leaves
1 lime, sliced, for garnish

Add lime juice, coconut, turmeric and salt to cooked rice. Set aside.

Heat ghee and fry mustard seeds until they pop. Add cashews, curry leaves and chillies and cook for 3 minutes, stirring. Combine with rice and coriander leaves and mix well. Cover and cook over low heat for 15 minutes to heat through. Garnish with lime slices.

Serves 6

1  Add ground cumin seeds, chillies, coconut and mangoes to rice

2  Fry curry leaves, mustard seeds and remaining chillies in ghee

3  When mustard seeds have popped, combine mixture with rice

Mango Pilau

# MANGO PILAU

1 kg long grain rice
1 teaspoon salt
½ teaspoon turmeric
1 teaspoon cummin seeds
6 red chillies, seeded and chopped
2 cups grated coconut
6 half-ripe mangoes, peeled and chopped
125 g ghee
3–4 curry leaves
2 teaspoons mustard seeds
2 red chillies, for garnish

Boil rice with salt and turmeric until cooked.

While rice is cooking, grind cummin seeds, 3 chillies and coconut together in food processor or blender. Mix with mangoes. Add to cooked rice with half the ghee. Set aside.

Heat remaining ghee and fry curry leaves, mustard seeds and remaining chillies until mustard seeds start to pop. Combine with rice mixture. Garnish with (but do not eat!) whole red chillies and serve immediately.

Serves 6

# DATE AND LENTIL PILAU

500 g long grain rice
1 cup lentils
250 g butter
1 cup warm water
1 small onion, finely chopped
250 g fresh dates, stoned
125 g dried apricots, chopped
½ cup blanched almonds, chopped
½ cup raisins

Boil rice until almost cooked. Cover lentils with water and cook for 20 minutes until soft. Dissolve half the butter in water over heat. Sauté onion in remaining butter until soft, add dates, apricots, almonds and raisins.

Pour ½ butter water into casserole then add, in layers, ⅓ of the rice, ½ of fruit mixture, ½ of the lentils, ⅓ of rice, remaining fruit mixture, remaining lentils then remaining rice and pour over the remaining butter-water. Cover with cloth then the lid and simmer over low heat for 30–40 minutes.

Serves 8

*Date and Lentil Pilau*

1  Combine dates with apricots, almonds and raisins

2  Add a layer of fruit mixture to layers of rice and butter water

3  Cover fruit with a layer of lentils and repeat the process

# SPINACH IN COCONUT MILK

1 cup grated fresh coconut
1 cup milk
1 kg spinach, shredded
1 onion, thinly sliced
1 teaspoon lemon juice
1 teaspon salt
freshly ground black pepper

Bring coconut and milk to the boil then set aside for 30 minutes. Press all liquid from coconut through fine sieve and discard pulp. Combine spinach with onion, lemon juice, salt, pepper and coconut milk, cover and simmer 10–15 minutes.

Serves 6

1   Add soaked ginger to coriander seeds, curry powder, flour and onions

2   Slowly add stock, always stirring

3   Stir in coconut, mixed fruit and cream and serve

Mixed Fruit Curry

# MIXED FRUIT CURRY

4–5 pieces crystallised ginger
hot water
2 onions, chopped
60 g butter
1 teaspoon crushed coriander seeds
1 tablespoon curry powder
1 tablespoon flour
500 mL chicken stock
2 teaspoons lemon juice
salt
freshly ground black pepper
3 cups grated coconut
4–5 cups chopped mixed fruits (melons, peaches, plums, grapes, bananas, apples, pears)
2–3 tablespoons cream

Cover ginger with hot water for a few minutes to remove sugar, drain, pat dry and chop.

Fry onions in butter until soft. Stir in ginger, coriander seeds, curry powder and flour and cook gently for 5 minutes. Gradually add stock, stirring rapidly. Bring to boil, add lemon juice and season to taste. Simmer for 30 minutes. Stir in coconut, prepared fruits and cream. Serve hot or cold with rice.

**Serves 4**

# APPLE AND ONION BAKE

6 onions, sliced
2 tablespoons ghee
10 thick slices tomato
½ cup breadcrumbs
4 apples, peeled and sliced
2 green chillies, seeded and finely chopped
2 tablespoons chopped coriander
1 cup hot chicken stock

Lightly fry onions in 1 tablespoon ghee. Remove with slotted spoon. Fry tomato slices. Drain off juices through strainer and reserve. Sauté breadcrumbs in remaining ghee to brown lightly. Grease baking dish and arrange onion, apple and tomato in alternate layers.

Put chillies, coriander and reserved juices into hot stock and pour over vegetables. Sprinkle breadcrumbs over top. Cover and bake at 190°C (375°F) for 30 minutes. Uncover and cook another 15 minutes.

Serves 4

Apple and Onion Bake
1   Sauté onions in ghee

2   Remove onions and sauté tomato slices

3   Layer onion, tomato and apple in a greased baking dish

# FRUIT STUFFING FOR CHICKEN

1 cup boiled rice
½ red capsicum, seeded and chopped finely
2 tablespoons raisins, snipped
1 tablespoon currants
3 tablespoons dried apricots, chopped
½ cup pecan nuts, roughly chopped
1 green apple, finely diced
1 teaspoon grated lemon rind
2 teaspoons salt
juice of 1 lemon
2 eggs, beaten
½ cup fresh breadcrumbs
½ coconut, grated
2 tablespoons chopped chives
1 tablespoon chopped parsley
cracked black pepper

Combine all ingredients together. Pack stuffing into cavity of 1.5 kg chicken. Close cavity and roast for 1½ hours until bird is golden and stuffing is cooked.

Makes 3–4 cups

*Curried Peaches*

# CURRIED PEACHES

2 tablespoons butter
½ red capsicum, seeded and sliced
½ green capsicum, seeded and sliced
1 tablespoon flour
1 tablespoon curry powder
1 cup milk
8 peaches, peeled, halved and stoned
¼ teaspoon paprika
2 bananas sliced
chopped chives for garnish

Melt butter and sauté red and green capsicum. Stir in flour and curry powder. Cook for 2 minutes, stirring. Pour in milk gradually, stirring rapidly until it comes to the boil. Add peaches and paprika and simmer for 20 minutes until peaches are tender. Add bananas and heat through.

Serve on bed of boiled rice, sprinkled with chopped chives.

Serves 4

# BANANA STUFFING FOR TURKEY OR GOOSE

6 ripe bananas, peeled and chopped
1 cup fresh breadcrumbs
½ cup shredded suet
½ cup chopped nuts
½ teaspoon dried mixed herbs
½ teaspon chopped parsley
1 egg, beaten
4 tablespoons water
salt
freshly ground black pepper

Combine all ingredients and season to taste. Pack stuffing into cavity of turkey or goose. Close cavity and roast until bird is golden and stuffing is cooked.

Makes 5–6 cups

*Fruity Flan (see recipe page 64)*

# DESSERTS

# FRUITY FLAN

## PASTRY:
3½ cups biscuit crumbs
½ cup ground hazelnuts
1 teaspoon grated orange rind
¾–1 cup melted butter

## FILLING:
8 egg yolks
1 cup sugar
5 tablespoons flour
1 tablespoon cornflour
600 mL milk, scalded
1 tablespoon orange liqueur

## TOPPING:
1 honeydew melon, scooped into balls
300 g muscat grapes
½ rockmelon, scooped into balls
2 guavas, sliced
½ kiwano (hornmelon)
1 strawberry

## GLAZE:
½ cup apricot jam
1 tablespoon orange liqueur

To make pastry, combine dry ingredients with butter. Press mixture into base and sides of 25 cm flan dish. Bake at 180°C (350°F) 10 minutes, remove and cool.

Combine yolks, sugar, flour and cornflour together in a bowl to form a smooth paste. Blend in scalded milk, return to saucepan and heat gently until thickened. Do not boil. Remove from heat and stir in liqueur. Allow to cool slightly, stirring occasionally. Pour filling into prepared pastry case and allow to set.

Arrange the fruit pieces decoratively over cooled filling.

To make glaze, warm apricot jam gently and stir in liqueur. Quickly brush hot glaze over fruit and allow to set.

Serve well chilled.

Serves 6–8

*pictured on previous page*

# FIGS IN OUZO

500 g figs
¼ cup Ouzo
cream

Remove stalks from figs and halve, but do not peel. Pour over Ouzo. Chill thoroughly and serve with cream.

Serves 4

# FRUIT SALAD IN COINTREAU

1 mango, peeled and chopped
¼–½ cup Cointreau
6 red plums, stoned and chopped
6 strawberries, quartered
3 apricots, stoned and chopped
pulp 3 passionfruit
1 lime, peeled and chopped
1 banana, peeled and sliced
1 kiwifruit, peeled and sliced
1 apple, cored and diced
1 rockmelon, seeded and scooped out with melon baller
1 guava, chopped

Marinate mango in small bowl with Cointreau for several hours. Purée in blender or food processor. Prepare remaining fruit, and combine with purée. Chill thoroughly.

Serves 6

# FRUIT SALAD IN CIDER

4 figs, sliced
2 kiwifruit, peeled and sliced
250 g green grapes, halved and seeded
2 apples, cored and sliced
2 pears, cored and sliced
1 pomegranate, diced
2 mandarins, segmented
2 tablespoons lemon juice
1 litre dry cider

Prepare all fruits, sprinkling lemon juice over apples and pears to prevent discoloration. Combine with cider and chill thoroughly.

Serves 8

*Fruit Salad in Cointreau*

# FEIJOA COMPOTE

¼ cup sugar
¾ cup water
¼ cup red wine
6 feijoas, peeled and halved lengthwise
1 tablespoon cornflour
1 tablespoon water

Dissolve sugar in water and wine over low heat. Add feijoas and simmer for a few minutes until cooked but not mushy. Lift feijoas out and arrange in serving dish. Mix cornflour and water to a smooth paste and stir into syrup. Bring to boil and cook, stirring, until thickened. Spoon over fruit.

**Serves 4**

*Feijoa Compote*

1 Dissolve sugar in water and wine over low heat

2 Add feijoas and simmer until cooked

3 Mix cornflour and water to a smooth paste and stir into syrup

# FRUIT IN VERMOUTH

½ cup sweet vermouth
¼ cup sugar
¼ teaspoon cinnamon
1 pineapple, cored and sliced
3 oranges, segmented
250 g green grapes, halved and seeded

Combine vermouth, sugar and cinnamon. Chill in refrigerator about 1 hour.

Place fruit in serving bowl and strain liquid over fruit. Chill at least 1 hour in refrigerator.

**Serves 6–8**

# STEWED PRICKLY PEARS

1 cup sugar
2½ cups water
few drops cochineal
16 prickly pears, peeled
juice 1 lemon
icing sugar

Boil sugar and water until thin syrup is formed. Add cochineal and stir well. Add pears and simmer for 3 minutes. Stir in lemon juice and chill thoroughly. Sprinkle with icing sugar. Serve with chilled custard.
**NOTE:** Gloves are essential for peeling prickly pears. Do not discard the seeds as they are edible.

**Serves 4**

# APRICOT CRISP

750 g apricots, halved and stoned
1¼ cups flour
1¼ cups brown sugar
pinch ground cloves
1 teaspoon cinnamon
185 g butter

Arrange apricots in greased, shallow ovenproof dish. Mix flour, sugar, cloves and cinnamon and rub in butter until mixture resembles coarse breadcrumbs. Sprinkle mixture evenly over apricots and pack down well. Bake at 190°C (375°F) for 30–40 minutes until crust is pale brown.

Serves 6

# CHERRY JANE

3 cups cherries, stoned
grated rind and juice ½ lemon
2½ cups stale cake crumbs
2 tablespoons melted butter
1 cup sugar

Mix cherries with lemon rind and juice. Mix half the cake crumbs with melted butter. Grease a pie plate and cover base with a layer of cherries. Sprinkle with sugar and top with unbuttered crumbs. Repeat layers, topping finally with the buttered crumbs. Cover and bake at 180°C (350°F) for 45 minutes. Remove cover and bake further 15 minutes.

Serves 4

*Stewed Prickly Pears*

# SPICED RHUBARB

500 g rhubarb, sliced
⅓ cup sultanas
⅓ cup raisins
⅓ cup currants
1 teaspoon mixed spices
1 teaspoon cinnamon
¼ cup brown sugar
½ cup apricot juice
1 cup sweet white wine

Mix rhubarb, dried fruits and spices and place in greased shallow ovenproof dish. Heat sugar in apricot juice until dissolved. Add wine and pour over fruit. Cover and bake at 135°C (270°F) for 30–35 minutes.

Serves 4

# NECTARINES WITH PECAN TOPPING

4 nectarines, halved and stoned
1 tablespoon rum
½ cup chopped pecans
2 tablespoons brown sugar
2 teaspoons butter, softened
2 teaspoons flour

Arrange nectarines cut side up in baking dish and sprinkle with rum. Mix pecans, brown sugar, butter and flour to a paste and divide between nectarines. Press gently to fill hollows; level top. Grill for 4 minutes until topping is brown and bubbly.

Serves 4

# FRUIT KEBAB WITH ORANGE CREAM

200 mL cream
6 tablespoons sour cream
1 tablespoon icing sugar, sifted
grated rind 1 orange
3 teaspoons cinnamon
4 tablespoons brown sugar
juice 1 orange
juice 1 lemon
8 peaches, peeled, halved and stoned
8 plums, halved and stoned
8 apricots, halved and stoned
2 pears, peeled, cored and quartered
4 bananas, peeled and cut in large slices
3 tablespoons brandy

To make orange cream, whip cream and fold in sour cream, icing sugar, orange rind and 1 teaspoon cinnamon. Cover and chill.

Stir brown sugar into orange and lemon juice and remaining cinnamon. Add all fruit and toss in sugar mixture until coated, using hands. Refrigerate for 1 hour.

Drain fruit and arrange on 8 long skewers.

Place a large sheet of foil in baking dish. Lay kebabs in single layer on foil then fold ends over to make a sealed parcel. Bake at 190°C (375°F) for 20–25 minutes.

Arrange kebabs on serving dish. Heat brandy, ignite and pour over fruit while still flaming. Serve with orange cream.

Serves 8

# STRAWBERRY SOUR CREAM DRESSING

2 cups sour cream
1 teaspoon salt
½ cup crushed strawberries

Mix salt into sour cream then fold in fruit. Serve with other fruit as a substitute for cream or custard, or serve with a tray of mixed fruits as a dip.

Makes 2½ cups

*Strawberry Sour Cream Dressing*

*Mango Brown Betty*

1  Place a layer of melted butter and coconut in a greased ovenproof dish

2  Top the butter and coconut with a layer of mangoes

3  Combine sugar and cinnamon and sprinkle over mangoes

# MANGO BROWN BETTY

3 tablespoons butter
1 cup grated fresh coconut
2 cups half-ripe, sliced mango
¾ cup brown sugar
1 teaspoon cinnamon
3 tablespoons liquid from coconut

Melt butter and mix with coconut. Place a layer of coconut in greased ovenproof dish then add a layer of mangoes. Mix sugar and cinnamon together and sprinkle over mangoes. Repeat layers ending with coconut. Spoon over coconut liquid. Bake at 180°C (350°F) for 1 hour until mangoes are soft. Serve with lime sauce (*see recipe following*).

Serves 6

## LIME SAUCE:

1 tablespoon cornflour
½ cup sugar
¼ cup cold water
¾ cup boiling water
2 tablespoons butter
2½ tablespoons lime juice

Combine cornflour and sugar and mix to a paste with cold water. Gradually stir mixture into boiling water, stirring continuously until thickened. Add butter and lime juice and mix well.

Makes 1½ cups

# BANANAS CARIBBEAN

6 bananas
¼ cup brown sugar
½ cup orange juice
grated rind 1 orange
¼ teaspoon cinnamon
¼ teaspoon nutmeg
½ cup sherry
30 g butter
4 tablespoons rum

Peel bananas and arrange in flat, greased baking dish. Combine brown sugar, orange juice and rind, cinnamon, nutmeg and sherry in saucepan. Heat to dissolve sugar then spoon over bananas. Dot with butter. Bake at 180°C (350°F) for 10–15 minutes until tender. Just before serving, heat rum, set alight and pour over bananas.

Serves 6

# RASPBERRY MARLOW

1½ cups raspberries
125 g marshmallows
⅓ cup fresh dates, thinly sliced
1 cup cream, whipped

Crush raspberries thoroughly. Heat with marshmallows over hot water until marshmallows melt. Add dates and refrigerate until cold. Fold in whipped cream and leave in freezer until frozen.

Serves 6

1   *Stir boiled milk into eggs*

2   *Add vanilla and gelatine and stir until dissolved*

3   *Cook guavas in lemon juice and sugar until just tender*

# GUAVA MOUSSE

1 tablespoon gelatine
2 tablespoons warm water
4 eggs
½ cup sugar
1 cup milk
1 teaspoon vanilla essence
500 g guavas, peeled and sliced
juice 1 lemon
1 tablespoon sugar
150 mL cream, whipped
1 guava and 1 kiwifruit, sliced for garnish

Dissolve gelatine in water. Beat eggs with sugar until light and fluffy. Boil milk and stir into eggs. Cook mixture over low heat until it coats the back of a wooden spoon. Add vanilla and gelatine and stir to dissolve. Leave in refrigerator until mixture thickens slightly.

Cook guavas in lemon juice and 1 tablespoon sugar until just tender. Cool slightly and purée in blender or food processor. Strain and discard seeds.

Fold cream into custard mixture with guavas. Taste and add more sugar if necessary. Pour into greased mould, cover and refrigerate for 6 hours until set. To serve, unmould onto serving platter and garnish with sliced guava and kiwifruit slices.

Serves 4

# PINEAPPLE SORBET

1 medium pineapple
2 limes
400 mL water
¾ cup caster sugar
mint sprigs for garnish

Cut pineapple in half lengthwise; leave leaves intact. Using grapefruit knife, remove the flesh, leaving shells whole for serving. Place pineapple shells in refrigerator until needed. Peel limes, removing white pith, cut in quarters. Purée lime and pineapple fruits in blender or food processor.

Simmer water and sugar for 8–10 minutes until sugar is dissolved and thin syrup forms. Allow to cool then add to pineapple mixture. Pour into freezer trays and freeze until set. Purée again in blender. Pour back into freezer trays, cover with foil and allow to refreeze.

When ready to serve, dip bottom of trays in hot water, tip out sorbet and cut into large dice. Pile sorbet into pineapple shells and serve. Garnish with mint sprigs.

Serves 6

*Pineapple Sorbet*
1 *Remove flesh using grapefruit knife*   2 *Peel limes and cut into quarters*   3 *Pour syrup into puréed fruit*

# BLACKCURRANT AND ORANGE ICE CREAM

250 g blackcurrants
finely grated rind and juice 1 orange
8 mint leaves
4 tablespoons brown sugar
300 mL yoghurt
2 eggs, separated
4–6 mint sprigs for garnish

Reserve a few blackcurrants for garnish. Purée remainder in blender or food processor. Add orange rind and juice, mint leaves, sugar, yoghurt and egg yolks and blend until smooth.

Leave in freezer until beginning to thicken and set. Beat egg whites until stiff and fold into ice cream. Freeze until half frozen then beat again. This prevents large ice crystals forming. Freeze until firm. Serve garnished with blackcurrants and mint leaves.

Serves 4

Tamarillo Ice Cream

1   Add tamarillos to simmering syrup

2   Bring cream to the boil and add yolks

3   Cool cream and then add to puréed
    tamarillos

# TAMARILLO ICE CREAM

1 cup sugar
1 cup water
4 tamarillos
450 mL cream
3 egg yolks, beaten

Boil sugar and water for 8–10 minutes until thin syrup is formed. Add tamarillos and simmer over low heat until just tender. Allow to cool, remove fruit, peel and discard skin. Purée fruit in food processor or blender and strain, discarding seeds.

Bring cream to the boil, add egg yolks and cook over low heat, stirring constantly until mixture coats back of a wooden spoon. Cool and combine with tamarillo purée and syrup. Pour into ice trays and freeze until nearly firm. Stir mixture then freeze until firm.

Makes 3 cups

1

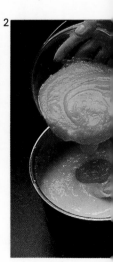

2

# SUN GLORY PAWPAW PUDDING

300 mL milk
⅓ cup semolina
2 tablespoons gelatine
2 tablespoons honey
juice and grated rind 1 lemon
juice and grated rind 1 orange
1 cup pawpaw pulp
150 mL cream
1 pawpaw
2 limes or lemons, thinly sliced

Boil milk, stir in semolina and cook 5 minutes. Blend gelatine and honey, stir into hot semolina mixture until dissolved. Flavour with lemon and orange rind and juice and stir in pawpaw pulp. Cool.

Whip cream and fold into mixture. Pour into greased 23 cm ring mould. Leave to set in refrigerator for 3–4 hours.

Turn pudding onto serving dish. Scoop out flesh from whole pawpaw with melon ball cutter and pile into centre.

Arrange lime or lemon slices around outside, overlapping each other.

Serves 6

*Sun Glory Pawpaw Pudding*
1  *Add lemon and orange rind and juice to semolina mixture*
2  *Stir in pawpaw*
3  *Fold in whipped cream*

# GOOSEBERRY BREAD PUDDING

4 cups gooseberries
1½ cups sugar
½ cup water
1½ cups fresh white breadcrumbs
2 tablespoons butter
¼ teaspoon salt
3 eggs, separated
2 tablespoons icing sugar

Cook gooseberries in sugar and water for 15–20 minutes until tender. Add breadcrumbs, butter, salt and egg yolks. Beat 1 egg white until stiff and fold into pudding. Pour into greased baking dish and bake at 180°C (350°F) for 20 minutes.

To make meringue, beat remaining two egg whites until peaks form, fold in icing sugar and beat until stiff. Pile meringue on top of pudding and return to oven for further 10–15 minutes until top is lightly browned.

Serves 6

# PLUM FLAN

## PASTRY:
1⅓ cups wholemeal flour
100 g butter
1 egg yolk
1–2 tablespoons milk

Rub butter into flour, add egg yolk and enough milk to form firm dough. Roll out and line 20 cm flan dish. Prick base a few times with fork.

## FILLING:
3 egg yolks
¼ cup honey
300 mL plain yoghurt
½ teaspoon powdered cinnamon
500 g small plums, halved and stoned
½ cup blanched almonds
1 tablespoon brown sugar

Beat yolks with honey, yoghurt and cinnamon. Pour into pastry case.

Arrange plums, cut side up in yoghurt mixture. Bake at 200°C (400°F) for 35–40 minutes, until custard is set. Place an almond in each plum, sprinkle with brown sugar and brown under hot grill.

Serves 6

# DATE SOUFFLÉ WITH ORANGE SAUCE

½ cup fresh dates, stoned
6 tablespoons flour
¼ cup softened butter
1 cup milk
2 tablespoons finely grated orange rind
3 eggs, separated
3 tablespoons sugar

Purée dates in blender or food processor. Mix with flour and butter. Heat milk until nearly boiling and gradually stir into date mixture. Cook over hot water about 5 minutes, stirring constantly. Add orange rind. Beat egg yolks until thick and beat in sugar gradually. Stir in hot mixture slowly. Cool. Fold in stiffly beaten egg whites, pour into greased soufflé dish, place in pan of hot water and bake at 160°C (325°F) for 1 hour until set. Serve with orange sauce (see recipe following).

Serves 6

## ORANGE SAUCE:

¼ cup sugar
1 tablespoon cornflour
1 cup orange juice
2 tablespoons finely grated orange rind
⅓ cup cream

Mix sugar and cornflour in saucepan. Add orange juice and rind and cook over medium heat, stirring constantly. Cover and cook over boiling water 10 minutes longer. Just before serving, stir in cream.

Makes 1½ cups

# MULBERRY PIE

## PASTRY:
1½ cups plain flour
1½ cups self-raising flour
2 tablespoons caster sugar
250 g butter
1 egg yolk
2–4 tablespoons cold water

## FILLING:
5 cups mulberries
½ cup water
1 cup sugar
3 tablespoons arrowroot
1 cup stewed apple, drained

To make pastry, sift flours and sugar together. Rub in butter until mixture resembles fine breadcrumbs. Mix in egg yolk and sufficient water to make a firm dough. Roll out half the pastry on lightly floured board and line 30 cm pie dish. Reserve remainder of pastry.

To make filling, cook mulberries with water and sugar for 15–20 minutes until soft. Strain through a coarse sieve, pushing gently with back of a spoon. Discard seeds. Return purée to saucepan. Mix arrowroot to paste with small amount of water, add to purée and cook, stirring constantly until thickened. Add apple and allow to cool. Spoon into pastry-lined pie dish and cover with remaining pastry. Crimp edges to seal. Bake at 230°C (450°F) for 10–15 minutes until browned then reduce to 200°C (400°F) and continue cooking for further 15–20 minutes.

Serves 6–8

# LEMON TART

½ quantity orange crust pastry (see recipe following)
6 eggs
⅔ cup sugar
juice 4 lemons
1½ cups cream
6 tablespoons butter, melted
1 lemon, sliced, for garnish

Roll out pastry on lightly floured board and line a 25 cm loose bottom flan tin. Cover pastry with foil, and place dried beans or uncooked rice on foil and bake at 200°C (400°F) for 5 minutes. Remove foil and beans and bake further 5 minutes. Allow to cool.

Beat eggs and sugar until light and lemon coloured. Stir in lemon juice, cream and butter. Pour into pastry case and bake at 160°C (325°F) for 45 minutes until firm. Spread with extra whipped cream and garnish with slices of lemon.

Serves 6

*Lemon Tart*

# ORANGE CRUST PASTRY:

2½ cups flour
½ teaspoon salt
½ cup cold unsalted butter
½ cup cold margarine
1 teaspoon grated orange peel
4 tablespoons cold orange juice

Sift flour with salt. Cut in butter and margarine; add orange peel. Rub with fingertips until the texture resembles coarse crumbs.

Using a knife, cut orange juice into flour mixture to form a soft dough. (Do not overwork.) Refrigerate 1 hour before using.

Makes enough for two 22 cm or 25 cm open tarts, or one 23 cm or 25 cm pie with lid.

75

# CAKES AND BISCUITS

## LEMON COCONUT SLICE

### BASE:
125 g soft margarine
¼ cup sugar
½ teaspoon vanilla essence
1 cup self-raising flour
½ cup grated coconut

### TOPPING:
¼ cup butter, softened
3 tablespoons condensed milk
juice and grated rind 1 lemon
1 cup icing sugar
1 cup grated coconut

Mix ingredients for base until well combined and press into Swiss roll tin. Bake at 180°C (350°F) for 20 minutes. While cooking, prepare topping. Combine ingredients for topping and spread over base while hot. Allow to set then cut into fingers.

## CRANBERRY CAKE

1 cup sugar
100 g butter
1 egg
2 cups flour
2 teaspoons baking powder
¼ teaspoon salt
½ teaspoon vanilla essence
6 tablespoons milk
125 g cranberries, halved
1–2 tablespoons caster sugar

Cream sugar and butter until light and fluffy. Beat in egg. Sift flour, baking powder and salt together. Mix vanilla essence with milk. Stir milk and flour alternately into butter mixture, beating well after each addition. Fold in cranberries. Turn into greased 20 cm square cake tin. Sprinkle with caster sugar and bake at 180°C (350°F) for 50 minutes until top springs back when lightly pressed.

*Lemon Coconut Slice*
1   *Mix ingredients for base*

2   *Press mixture into Swiss roll tin*

3   *Combine ingredients for topping*

# COCOA AND PASSIONFRUIT CAKE

1 cup sugar
2 tablespoons butter
1 egg, beaten
½ teaspoon bicarbonate of soda
2 tablespoons milk
1½ cups self-raising flour
pinch salt
1 tablespoon cocoa
pulp 3 passionfruit

## FILLING:

1 teaspoon cocoa
pulp 2 passionfruit

## PASSIONFRUIT ICING:

1 cup icing sugar
pulp 2 passionfruit

Cream sugar and butter, add egg. Dissolve bicarbonate of soda in milk and stir into mixture. Sift flour, salt and cocoa and fold into mixture with passionfruit pulp.

Bake in greased slab tin at 180°C (350°F) for 15 minutes. Turn out and cut in half. Coat one piece with filling. Place other piece of cake on top and ice with passionfruit icing.

# FIG AND APPLE CAKE

125 g butter, softened
1 cup sugar
3 eggs, beaten
2 tablespoons shredded coconut
3 cups self-raising flour, sifted
grated rind ½ lemon
4 medium figs, peeled and finely chopped
1 small apple, peeled, cored and grated

Cream butter and sugar together. Beat in eggs. Stir in coconut, lemon rind, figs and apple. Fold in flour and pour into well greased 20 cm square or round cake tin. Bake at 180°C (350°F) for 40 minutes. Reduce heat to 150°C (300°F) and bake further 20–30 minutes or until cake is cooked.

When cold, ice cake with passionfruit icing (*see previous recipe*).

# MANGO FILLED ROLL

3 eggs, separated
½ cup caster sugar
¾ cup flour
2 teaspoons baking powder
2 tablespoons hot milk
2 tablespoons caster sugar

## FILLING:

1 cup cream
1 cup mashed mango
1 tablespoon icing sugar, sifted
1 teaspoon whisky

Grease and line Swiss roll tin with greased greaseproof paper. Beat egg whites until stiff. Gradually beat in sugar until mixture becomes thick and glossy. Beat in yolks one at a time. Sift flour and baking powder and fold into mixture with the hot milk. Pour mixture into tin and smooth the surface. Bake at 220°C (450°F) for 10 minutes. Turn cake out onto a sheet of greaseproof paper sprinkled with caster sugar.

Roll cake up and allow to cool. Whip cream till thick. Fold in mango, sugar and whisky and chill. Unroll cake and spread with cream.

Roll up and chill before serving.

*Fig and Apple Cake*

1   *Beat egg into creamed butter and sugar*

2   *Stir in lemon rind and pineapple*

3   *Sift flours and fold into mixture*

*Hawaiian Moments*

# HAWAIIAN MOMENTS

90 g butter
½ cup sifted icing sugar
1 egg
2 tablespoons grated pineapple
½ teaspoon grated lemon rind
1 tablespoon grated coconut
1 cup flour
3 tablespoons cornflour

Cream butter and icing sugar until light and fluffy. Beat in egg. Stir in pineapple, lemon rind and coconut. Sift flour and cornflour and fold into butter mixture. Drop teaspoonfuls of the mixture on a greased tray and bake at 180°C (350°F) for 10 minutes. When cold drizzle with melted chocolate or favourite fruity icing.

Makes 24

# COCONUT CAKE

125 g butter
1 cup sugar
2 eggs
1½ cups self-raising flour, sifted
1½ cups grated coconut
⅓ cup coconut milk
2 teaspoons sugar

Cream butter and sugar until light and fluffy. Beat in eggs. Fold in flour and 1 cup of grated coconut with coconut milk. Pour mixture into greased 26 cm x 16 cm slice tin. Mix remaining ½ cup coconut with sugar and sprinkle over mixture. Bake for 45–50 minutes at 190°C (375°F).

# BANANA SNAPS

¼ cup butter
⅓ cup sugar
1 egg, separated
¾ cup flour
1 teaspoon baking powder
½ teaspoon cinnamon
½ cup sliced banana
¼ teaspoon vanilla essence
extra sugar

Cream butter and sugar, add beaten egg yolk. Sift flour with baking powder and cinnamon and fold into mixture. Stir in banana and vanilla essence. Roll out thinly. Brush over with egg white, sprinkle lightly with sugar and cut into squares. Bake at 190°C (375°F) for 10 minutes.

Makes 12

1 Beat sugar, margarine and egg

2 Stir in apples

3 Mix thoroughly together and add nuts

Apple Bars

# APPLE BARS

1 cup brown sugar
¼ cup margarine
1 egg
2 cups chopped apples
2 cups flour
1 teaspoon bicarbonate of soda
1 teaspoon cinnamon
½ teaspoon nutmeg
¼ teaspoon salt
½ cup chopped nuts

Beat sugar, margarine and egg together until light and fluffy. Stir in apples. Sift flour with bicarbonate of soda, cinnamon, nutmeg and salt and mix well into apple mixture with nuts. Spread in greased 23 cm square pan and bake at 180°C (350°F) for 40–45 minutes. Cool in pan. Top with lemon frosting (*see recipe following*) and chop into squares.

Makes 9–12

## LEMON FROSTING:

2–3 teaspoons lemon juice
1 teaspoon grated lemon rind
⅔ cup icing sugar
pecan nuts and orange peel, shredded, for decoration

Mix all ingredients together and spread over apple bars using wet spatula. Decorate with whole pecan nuts and shredded orange peel.

# SCONES, MUFFINS AND BREAD

## PAWPAW SCONES

2 cups self-raising flour
½ teaspoon salt
1 tablespoon butter
¼ cup sugar
1 teaspoon grated lemon rind
¾ cup mashed pawpaw pulp

Sift flour and salt and rub in butter. Add sugar and mix well. Mix to soft dough with lemon rind and pawpaw. Turn onto floured board and knead lightly. Press out to 1.25 cm thickness, cut rounds with floured scone-cutter; place close together on greased oven tray. Bake at 250°C (500°F) 10–12 minutes. Turn onto wire rack and cover with cloth to cool.

Makes 10–12

## WHOLEMEAL AVOCADO MUFFINS

1 egg
1 avocado, peeled, seeded and chopped
2 tablespoons caster sugar
1 cup wheatgerm
1 cup wholemeal flour
3 teaspoons baking powder
½ teaspoon salt
1 cup milk

Beat egg and avocado together. Sift sugar, wheatgerm, flour, baking powder and salt and fold into avocado mixture with milk until just combined. Pour batter into 12 greased muffin tins. Bake at 200°C (400°F) for 20 minutes.

Makes 12 muffins or 16 cup cakes.

*Pawpaw Scones*
1   *Sift flour and rub in butter*

2   *Mix in pawpaw and lemon rind*

3   *Cut rounds with floured scone cutter*

# MANGO BREAD

2 cups flour
1½ cups sugar
2 teaspoons bicarbonate of soda
2 teaspoons cinnamon
½ teaspoon salt
3 eggs
1½ cups diced mangoes
1 cup salad oil
½ cup grated fresh coconut
½ cup raisins
½ cup chopped macadamia nuts
1 teaspoon vanilla essence

Sift flour, sugar, bicarbonate of soda, cinnamon and salt. Add to remaining ingredients and mix well. Pour into two 19 cm x 9 cm or one 23 cm x 12 cm greased loaf tins. Bake at 180°C (350°F) for 55 minutes until bread shrinks away slightly from sides of tin.

*above right: Banana Bread*
*below: Mango Bread*

# BANANA BREAD

125 g butter
1½ cups brown sugar
1 egg
3 ripe bananas, mashed
2 cups flour
1 teaspoon bicarbonate of soda
½ teaspoon salt

Cream butter and sugar until light and fluffy. Beat in egg. Add bananas. Sift dry ingredients together and stir into mixture. Pour into a greased 19 cm x 9 cm loaf tin and bake for 45–60 minutes at 180°C (350°F) until bread shrinks away slightly from sides of tin.

# BERRY MUFFINS

3 cups flour
½ cup sugar
1 tablespoon baking powder
1 teaspoon salt
½ cup brown sugar
½ cup butter, melted
3 eggs
1 cup milk
1–1½ cups berries in season
icing sugar

Sift flour, sugar, baking powder and salt into bowl. Stir in brown sugar. Combine butter, eggs and milk and stir into dry ingredients until just blended. If large berries such as strawberries are used, cut into dice. Fold in berries very lightly and carefully. Spoon into greased muffin tins until two-thirds full. Bake at 200°C (400°F) for 20 minutes until browned. Sprinkle with icing sugar while hot. Serve hot with butter.

Makes 20–24

*Fig and Passionfruit Jam*
*(see recipe page 85)*

# JAMS, PRESERVES AND CHUTNEYS

1  *Cut cross in pointed end of persimmon and peel back skin*

2  *Cook pulp and sugar over low heat*

3  *Stir in lemon juice, rind and pineapple*

# PERSIMMON JAM

4 ripe persimmons
2 cups sugar
1 tablespoon lemon juice
½ cup grated pineapple
shredded peel 1 lemon

Cut a cross in pointed ends of persimmons. Peel back skin. Discard skin and stem end. Combine pulp with sugar and cook over low heat 15 minutes, stirring constantly until thickened and clear. Do not boil. Stir in lemon juice, pineapple and lemon rind. Pour into warm, sterilised jars. Seal when cool.

# FIG AND PASSIONFRUIT JAM

500 g figs, sliced
1 cup passionfruit pulp
sugar

Boil figs and passionfruit together for 10 minutes. Measure and allow 1 cup sugar to each cup fruit. Boil again until a little tested on a cold saucer shows signs of setting. Pour into warm, sterilised jars and seal when cold.

*pictured on page 83*

# BANANA AND PINEAPPLE JAM

1 pineapple, peeled and grated
6 bananas, peeled and sliced
1 kg sugar

Simmer fruit until tender. Add sugar and boil until thick. Pour into warm, sterilised jars and seal when cold.

# GRAPEFRUIT MARMALADE

3 grapefruit, thinly sliced
3 litres water
3 kg sugar
1 teaspoon salt
1 teaspoon cream of tartar

Cover grapefruit with water and allow to stand at least 12 hours. Cover and cook over low heat until tender. Leave till next day. Bring slowly to the boil, stir in sugar, salt and cream of tartar. Stir until sugar dissolves. Boil rapidly until marmalade jells when tested on cold saucer. Bottle while hot in warm, sterilised jars. Seal when cold.

# LOQUAT JELLY

loquats
sugar
lemons

Cut loquats and remove seeds. Cover with cold water and boil for 2 hours. Strain and measure the juice. To every litre allow 250 g sugar and juice of ½ lemon. Bring to the boil, stirring, then simmer slowly for 2 hours until it forms a jelly.

# PLUM BUTTER

1 kg plums
sugar
1 teaspoon ground cinnamon

Barely cover plums with water, cover and cook very slowly until tender. Push through sieve, discarding stones. Measure purée and for every 2½ cups add 500 g sugar. Slowly heat, stirring, until sugar dissolves. Add cinnamon and boil for about ¾ hour until a spoon drawn across pan leaves a clean line behind it. Pour into warm sterilised jars and cover.

*Feijoa and Guava Jelly*

1   *Cut up fruit roughly*

2   *Push cooked fruit through sieve*

3   *Bring juice to the boil and add sugar*

# FEIJOA AND GUAVA JELLY

1.25 kg feijoas
1 kg apples, cored
500 g guavas
sugar

Cut up all fruit roughly and cover with water. Boil for 1 hour until mushy. Push through a sieve, or strain through a jelly bag or muslin overnight. Measure juice and allow ¾ cup sugar to each cup of juice. Bring juice to the boil, add sugar, stirring until dissolved. Boil rapidly for 10 minutes or until a few drops tested on a cold saucer show signs of setting. Pour into warm, sterilised jars and seal when cold.

*Plum Butter*

# BRANDIED CUMQUATS

1.5 kg cumquats
2 kg sugar
3 litres water
300 mL brandy

Cut stalks to within an eighth of an inch from the fruit. Do not use fruit without stalks. Prick each cumquat several times with a darning needle making sure the needle penetrates the centre. Boil sugar and water rapidly for 15–20 minutes to make a syrup. Gently lower fruit into syrup. Cover with wire rack to stop fruit floating. Leave for 24 hours.

Drain fruit, reserving syrup. Boil syrup for 10–12 minutes to evaporate juices. While still boiling, return fruit to syrup, remove from heat, cover and leave for a further 24 hours. Repeat again for four more days until fruit becomes glacé in appearance and does not float.

Put fruit in jars, cover with syrup and brandy and leave to stand for 3 weeks before using.

*Peach Brandy*

1    *Peel and slice peaches*

2    *Crack stones to extract kernels*

3    *Add spices, sugar and brandy*

# PEACH BRANDY

500 g ripe peaches
500 mL brandy
1 cup sugar
1 piece cinnamon stick
5 cloves
¼ teaspoon ground mace

Cover peaches with boiling water for a few minutes, drain and peel. Cut each peach into 8 segments and remove stones. Extract kernels by splitting stones with nutcracker or hammer. Bruise kernels by squashing under flat blade of knife and put in large mixing bowl with fruit and remaining ingredients. Mix well and pour into prepared jars. Store in cool, dark cupboard for at least 3 months before opening.

NOTE: Peaches may be served as dessert.

# TAMARILLO CHUTNEY

12 tamarillos, blanched and diced
250 g apples, peeled, cored and thinly sliced
250 g onion, finely chopped
500 g brown sugar
2 teaspoons mixed spice
2 teaspoons salt
pinch cayenne pepper
300 mL white vinegar

Bring all ingredients to the boil then simmer for 45 minutes until thick, stirring occasionally. Pour into warm, sterilised jars and seal.

*Tamarillo Chutney*

# APRICOT CHUTNEY

1 kg apricots, halved and stoned
2 onions, thinly sliced
2 cups brown sugar
¾ cup sultanas
1 tablespoon salt
1 teaspoon coriander seeds
½ teaspoon ground ginger
250 mL wine vinegar

Simmer all ingredients together until apricots are soft — about 15–20 minutes. Transfer apricots to warm, sterilised jars. Boil rest of chutney until it is thick and syrupy. Pour over apricots and seal.
**NOTE:** Peaches may be substituted for apricots.

# BRANDIED GRAPE PRESERVE

1⅓ cups red wine vinegar
1½ cups red wine
¾ cup sugar
3 cloves
4 sticks cinnamon
1 kg black grapes, seeded
2 tablespoons brandy

Bring vinegar, wine, sugar, cloves and cinnamon sticks to the boil. Simmer for 15 minutes until syrupy. Remove cinnamon sticks. Add brandy and pour over grapes. Put into warm, sterilised jars and seal.
**NOTE:** Serve with terrines, game birds and venison.

# PEACH CHUTNEY

5 kg peaches, peeled, halved and stoned
1.25 kg sugar
250 g salt
30 g allspice
30 g cloves
15 g peppercorns, ground
30 g garlic, peeled and chopped
2 x 750 mL bottles white vinegar

Boil all ingredients together for 3 hours or until thick. Pour into warm, sterilised jars and seal.
**NOTE:** Plums may be substituted for peaches.

# WATERMELON RIND PICKLES

1 kg watermelon rind
¼ cup salt
1 litre water
2 cups white vinegar
2 cups water
4 cups sugar
1 stick cinnamon
1 teaspoon whole cloves
1 teaspoon allspice
1 lemon, thinly sliced

Cut watermelon rind into 2.5 cm x 5 cm x 1.3 cm pieces. Soak overnight in salt and water. Drain and wash well in fresh water. Drain and cook in fresh water until liquid is clear.

Combine remaining ingredients and boil for 5 minutes. Add rind a few pieces at a time so boiling doesn't stop. Cook until clear. Cover and allow to stand overnight.

Remove rind, bring syrup to boil, pour over rind and leave overnight. Repeat twice (3 nights in all).

Pack rind in warm, sterilised jars; bring syrup to boil and pour over.

# APPLE AND PEAR MUSTARD

pared rind 1 lemon
½ cup white grape juice
1 cup dry white wine
2 sticks cinnamon
375 g Granny Smith (green cooking) apples, peeled, cored and diced
375 g pears, peeled, cored and diced
150 g white grapes, peeled and seeded
200 g Dijon mustard
½ teaspoon dark mustard seeds

Place lemon rind, grape juice, wine and cinnamon sticks in saucepan, bring to the boil and simmer for 5 minutes. Discard lemon rind and simmer for further 5 minutes. Discard cinnamon sticks. Add fruit and simmer for 15–20 minutes until just tender. Carefully blend in mustard and seeds and simmer for further 2–3 minutes. Pour into warm, sterilised jars and seal.

*Apple and Pear Mustard*
1    *Add fruit to wine mixture and simmer*
2    *Stir in mustard and seeds*
3    *Pour into warm, sterilised jars*

# BEVERAGES

# PARTY PUNCH

2 tablespoons tea
600 mL boiling water
grated rind and juice 3 oranges
grated rind and juice 3 lemons
1 cup sugar
1 cup water
1 cup fruit cordial
pulp 6 passionfruit
1 orange, thinly sliced
1 lemon, thinly sliced
1 lime, thinly sliced
mint sprigs
ice cubes
1 litre bottle ginger ale
1 litre bottle soda water

Make tea with boiling water; infuse for 5 minutes then strain and cool. Simmer grated orange and lemon rinds with sugar and water for 5 minutes. Strain into tea. Add cordial and passionfruit, then chill until needed. Empty into punch bowl, add remaining ingredients.

Makes 3 litres

# PASSIONFRUIT PUNCH

1 cup sugar
½ cup water
1 cup orange juice
1 cup lemon juice
1 cup passionfruit pulp
ice cubes
1 bottle sparkling white wine
orange and lemon slices for garnish

Bring sugar and water to the boil, stirring constantly. Continue to cook for 5 minutes then allow to cool. Add orange and lemon juices and passionfruit. Chill until needed. To serve, place a quantity of ice cubes in punch bowl, pour syrup over ice, pour in wine and garnish with orange and lemon slices.

Makes 1.5 litres

*Party Punch*

*previous page:* Mixed Fruit Cup (*see recipe page* 95)

# WATERMELON PINEAPPLE PUNCH

1.5 kg piece watermelon, peeled, seeded and chopped
1 ¼ cups pineapple juice
1 cup lime juice
1 cup vodka
sugar to taste
1–2 limes, thinly sliced, for garnish

Purée watermelon in blender or food processor. Force through a fine sieve, discarding any remaining pulp. Stir in pineapple and lime juices and vodka. Add sugar to taste. Chill well and serve garnished with lime slices.

Makes 1.5 litres

94

# ALOHA PUNCH

⅓ cup sugar
⅓ cup water
8 whole cloves
1 stick cinnamon
3 cups pineapple juice
3 cups orange juice
⅓ cup lemon juice
2 tablespoons rum
1 litre bottle ginger ale
ice cubes

Combine sugar, water, cloves and cinnamon stick and simmer for 5 minutes. Allow to cool then strain into fruit juices. Chill thoroughly. To serve, mix with rum, ginger ale and ice cubes.

Makes 2.5 litres

# MULBERRY FRUIT CUP

500 g ripe mulberries
250 g sugar
2 litres water
juice 1 lemon
strip lemon rind
sherry (optional)

Boil all ingredients except sherry together for 20 minutes. Strain and chill thoroughly. Serve with 1 teaspoon sherry per glass, if liked, and ice cubes.

Makes 2.5 litres

*left: Watermelon Pineapple Punch*

# PASSIONA

1½ cups water
1½ cups sugar
1½ teaspoons tartaric acid
pulp 48 passionfruit

Boil water, sugar and tartaric acid until sugar dissolves. While still boiling add passionfruit, beating with a fork for 3 minutes to extract all the juice. Pour into bowl, mix well and bottle.

To serve, add a small quantity to a glass of water or soda water. If well corked it will keep for some time.

Makes 600 mL

# MIXED FRUIT CUP

1 pawpaw, peeled and seeded
2 bananas, sliced
1 litre water
1 cup sugar
1 cup orange juice
½ cup lemon juice
pulp 12 passionfruit
2 x 750 mL bottles soda water
ice cubes
10 strawberries, sliced
1 orange, thinly sliced
mint leaves

Purée pawpaw and bananas in food processor or blender. Boil water and sugar, stirring for 8–10 minutes until sugar dissolves and thin syrup is formed. Immediately pour onto orange and lemon juices. Add puréed fruit and passionfruit. Chill until needed.

To serve, add soda water and ice cubes and garnish with strawberries, orange slices and mint leaves.

Makes 3 litres

*Mixed Fruit Cup —pictured on page 91*

1   *Pour syrup into orange and lemon juices*   2   *Add puréed fruit*   3   *Stir in passionfruit and chill thoroughly*

# Index

Printed in Singapore